"Darlene is one of those people she wants to share the joy she play she shares this love and jo the rebirth of the child in us all to play again!"

—Mischelle Ellis Farnsworth, Salt Lake City, UT, Registered Nurse

"Hey you! The one standing there like a deer in the headlights. All because someone asked you what you enjoy doing. Blinking like that because you forgot. Because you've been so busy taking care of everyone else. Don't worry, now. Mama Darlene has got you covered. She's here to re-introduce you to the world of fun. That world you inhabited when you were young. Before all those responsibilities. Remember? Run along now. It's time to play. Go on. It's ok."

—Ann Sheybani, founder of Starting Over, and author of *Things Mama Never Taught Me*

"I love this book so much my inner child is jumping around ready to play! Everyone in the world has an inner children waiting for this book."

—Anusuya A. Goldbrunner, German primary school teacher and Social education worker

"If you like the works of Abraham-Hicks, Gary Chapman (*The Five Love Languages*), Steve Pavlina, or Sark, then there's a good chance you will absolutely LOVE Play Is The New Way. This delightful book provides an abundance of playful ideas and concepts I had never thought of before! I plan to keep rereading this book for inspiration to play and celebrate as often as possible."

—Phoenix Littlefoot Huber, Phoenix, AZ

"This book will resonate with anyone lucky enough to read it. Darlene took the simple and transformed it into a tool that makes so much sense."

—Dan Olivas, Real Estate Broker at Dan Olivas and Associates El Paso, TX

"Darlene Navarre has brilliantly extracted mind fullness virtues in a simple non-diluted language. A language that is concise yet flows when you engage in the lessons provided in this new life science manual towards embracing the mind set of integration for self from self! A great way to abandon fears by empowering the reader to challenge the most insidious robber of joy our old patterns and belief! I feel lighter each day!!"

Thomas Schiffer, Owner of Grey Block Pizza, Los Angeles, CA

"Darlene's book has transformed my life in a deep and magical way. My new and improved playful attitude enabled me to attract opportunities, relationships, health and even money that wouldn't have come into my life otherwise!"

Karen Bell, KtotheB.com, London, ON, Canada

THE BOOK THAT CREATED
A PLAY EXPLOSION FOR ADULTS...

...by the woman thousands turn to, to remind them to play.

Today, right this minute, if someone said to you, "Go outside and play!" like your Mother used to, what would you do? Would you be stumped as to finding something to do? Do you remember how it felt to be free of any restraint that prevented you from going outside and finding a favorite pastime either by yourself or with friends? How long has it been since you felt that freedom? That uplifting sense of adventure and the "What if I do. . ." of life? Why does the word "play" stir up ambivalence?

Are we so programmed with "doing" that it is nearly impossible to just "be"? Why do we feel guilty even thinking about "playing" certain that we would only be wasting time because we have more important things to accomplish? As our society has become supposedly more sophisticated, we have left a trail of simple joys behind. I remember the neighborhood where I grew up and we played in all sorts of ways: board games, cards, "pretend," camping, dress up, physical activities, such as riding bikes, skating, and so much more.

The most amazing thing that I realized later in life is that the whole neighborhood in its own way had participated in what we did. We had our own Neighbor Watch before it even became official! Because many mothers stayed at home during my childhood, they became the observers of their children and those in the neighborhood and got to passively play with us. Sometimes, they actively participated by playing "ball" with us or filling in as a player in various games. Families and neighbors were engaged with our play. But, it was unified play in the sense that seems to be lacking today. It was unstructured play where one played with those in the neighborhood; they didn't have to be your "best friend." You accepted those in your neighborhood simply because they lived in the neighborhood – no matter their color, race, religion. It did not require scooting your child in the car and driving five miles to gather a kid to bring home for your child to have playtime. So where does that leave us?

Times have changed and as important as it is to socialize with others, we have learned that the ability to do so comes from within. Since everything is energy and we are the creators of our own lives, it is essential that we begin to understand that life is meant to be enjoyed and not turned into the drudgery that most of us make it into. In The Play Book, you will realize the importance of play and what that playful energy creates, not only for you, but those around you for energy is infinite.

Darlene Navarre, the author of this "must read" book is someone very special. I was instantly drawn to her when I met her. She is beautiful in all ways with clear, intelligent blue eyes that light up when speaking to you. Without using words, like a fairy god mother, she made me believe in possibilities and the idea that if I shifted my energies, my dreams would come true. She has a mischievous smile that fills her face when she says, "What if you switched it to…" and suddenly you see how that idea becomes special and whatever concern you are working on seems effortless now. She is the Lady of Play who makes you want to run to get paper and crayons out to draw funny pictures to hang on the refrigerator just like yesteryear.

Darlene is a gift to us all and once you read her delightful, life-changing book, you will understand just how much of a gift she is. Darlene leads us through her stories and some of the stories of others showing us how important it is to shift our thoughts and conduct of how we spend our time to always include "play" and the positive energy that creates. This book is filled with ideas of many ways that we can have fun that most of us have forgotten or left by the wayside. More importantly, she reminds us and explains how that positive energy brings back to us the things that we want to manifest in our lives. All good things are waiting for us to claim them and it is possible to do so with a little guidance and understanding of how we can create the energy that allows us to receive them. Darlene shares with us step by step how to do this. Her book is a marvel allowing us to view life differently that will bring you joy, laughter, a sense of well-being, a direction for individual and collective success and a renewal in the goodness of life. Once you read this exceptional book, you will be able to allow yourself to be silly and vulnerable as a human being and simply have fun. So keep reading her book as I have done; see for yourself.

In other words, "Tag! You're it!" (See what I mean).

Joan Peck

DEDICATION

This Play Book is dedicated to:

My mom, Glenna Smith Carter - the person who always continued to play all the way through till the end of her physical life.

My grandmomma Smith - for always loving, believing in and understanding me when no one else "got me." You did and always have.

Five amazing beings who came through my body and are my biggest teachers and inspiring beings: Danyell, Marc, Breeana, Mitchel, and Carter - the best teachers of play who continue to inspire me.

Blake for all the support that allowed me to follow my passion and purpose and for being the one who reminded me to PLAY.

All the others amazing players whom have shown up in my life, my friends, family and, of course, YOU!

May you absorb this book into every fiber of your being because every day in every way there is always an opportunity to PLAY!

PLAY IS THE NEW WAY!

Create a Healthy, Wealthy and Joyful Life

Darlene Navarre

INSPIRATION
BOOKS

PLAY IS THE NEW WAY!
Create A Healthy, Wealthy and Joyful Life
by Darlene Navarre

ISBN-13: 978-0615606880
ISBN-10: 0615606881

Inspiration Books Publishing
PO Box 530063
Henderson, NV 89053 U.S.A.

Website http://www.GoPlazy.com

Edited by Teresa Kneller Griffith, FlowNorth.ca,
    LoveYourSkeletons.com
Cover painting by Karen Bell, www.KtotheB.com
Layout by Clark Kenyon, www.camppope.com

CONTENTS

ABOUT THE AUTHOR

DARLENE NAVARRE

Darlene Navarre's creative purpose and driving obsession with play will inspire you and remind you of how fun life can really be! She continues to be an example of how "playing" can improve your health, support you to feel more joyful, and live a more fulfilling life easily just by following your bliss. Her playful approach has already inspired thousands and continues to touch the lives of those she meets daily.

As the mother of 5 children, she has a genuine love of people of all ages! You automatically feel her joy and caring nature from the moment she greets you with her great big smile and loving eye contact. Many have expressed how she is able to bring out the best in them because she practices seeing and believing in the best of them. She is a friend to all and strongly believes that *"Strangers are just friends I haven't met yet!"* and you feel this from the second you talk with her because you instantly feel like her best friend.

For the past 21 years, Darlene has continually studied and researched health, wellness and the "power of one" ability to heal yourself. After spending the 1990s playing in the fitness industry, personal training, and instructing playful Spin Classes, she turned to the food and diet platform. She took her love of cooking and transformed herself into a fresh raw food chef. Due to the lack of Living and Raw Foods education available at the time, she started her own successful Raw Food preparation education classes called "Keep It Simple Sweetie, Just Play With Your Food". Later, she went on to own and operate The Garden Spot, a private raw food catering service. By popular demand she began personal one-on-one health coaching and launched www.Raw-Food-Diet-Inspiration.com in 2009, a free on-line health resource to share raw food recipes, inspiring others to start *playing* with fresh foods and become healthy in the process.

Taking play from the kitchen to all areas of health and happiness, Darlene was moved to create GoPlazy Inc, a playfully fun, experiential company dedicated to providing Play Shoppes (workshops) designed to inspire and remind women and men to play again! Those who find themselves unhappy, stressed and bored find laughter, joy and fun at a Play Shoppe. After all, *every day in every way there is always an opportunity to play* is the motto she practices and leads others to strive for daily.

Darlene's philosophies include creating your life on purpose, living passionately and feeling "Fantabulous" as much as possible. She has discovered that this continues to attract more of all the good stuff we all want. Her specialty is creative expression by being fun and *flirting* with the Universe and everyone in it. In her playful approach, she has uncovered the benefits of true health, wellness, wealth and deep meaning of this human experience we are all in. . . sit back, relax, have fun and Go Play!

PREFACE

The Beginning of a Play Dream

As I began writing The Play Book that first morning, I found myself more and more excited about the prospect of supporting you to relieve and release stress by simply and easily turning your attention toward having fun and playing. And now, I am filled with pure joy as I imagine you reading this book — what you may take away from it, how it will benefit your life and, hopefully, how it will fill a need, answer a question, or offer a solution to support you to live your life more fully by playing! As I look further into the deepest space in my heart, I dream that this book will touch your life in such a way you will free your playful spirit and become childlike again.

Being in touch and in tune with your innate playful nature will unlock your imagination and creativity, allowing you to manifest a life that is easy, fun and playful. As children, we learn and do everything from eating to talking to walking through play. Today, most of us are still enjoying these marvelous basic skills, and yet are we continuing to play? Can you imagine how different your life would be and how you would feel if you began to add play into a small portion of your day when doing simple tasks such as the dishes or getting ready in the morning?

Now, more than ever, we all need to have fun and play. Our world is rapidly expanding and moving quickly. Stress levels in the majority of people's lives are at an all-time high. Getting things done takes much more effort than ever and our health, happiness and well-being is taking a hit. Today we have more educational opportunities, medical support, information and money yet still most of us feel as if we have a more stressful, lower quality of life than ever as we struggle to keep up, compete, and get it all done.

Take a deep breath and let me ask you: as a child, didn't you learn, and live life much easier with much less effort when you played? Perhaps you will remember a time when you were having so much fun that "time just flew by"? If you have forgotten your childhood, or feel as if you were never given the chance to play as a child or even allowed yourself to play as an adult, then I invite you to go observe babies or young children. What you will most likely witness is that even in the worst circumstances such as war or abuse, children WILL release stress, learn and grow by playing.

Play IS the new way although play is not really new — we are all born with imaginations, the desire to have fun and the ability to play in some form or fashion. We truly are the creators of our reality and as such, isn't it about time you created your life to be easy and fun? Eventually, your health and happiness will depend on your ability to surrender and let go, allowing your playful spirit to surface… or perhaps sadness, illness, tragedy or dis-ease will be your chosen path. You do have a choice to create, design and manifest the life you DO want to live. The power lies within you and I welcome you in this moment to dance, hop and play along as you explore, uncover and remember ways to stop and GO PLAY again!

ACKNOWLEDGMENTS

Without the unconditional support and love of my family, friends, and editors of this book, it would not have been as beautiful and in your hands as it is today.

Special thanks and acknowledgement to my partner in print Teresa Kneller Griffith. She completely understood what I wanted to say and rewrote it so beautifully! She believed in the vision from the beginning and continues be an example of fun and play in her life, while inspiring others along the way!

For all her last minute editing, love and continued nudging, Joan Peck. You are such a kindred spirit in my life! Thank you so much as I know we will continue to edit and print books for the rest of our days!

Heart hugs and love to my supportive soul sisters, Annetta Spotten Olson and Jeannetta Spotten Wright. You both are doubly a big part of the fun and love in my life. Thank you both for always accepting and loving me unconditionally, and for always pointing me toward the best path, all the while drawing out my greatest gifts and strengths! I feel so blessed to have manifested you two!

Dixie Story, the woman who has continued to be my friend, pseudo mother and spiritual inspirer, I will continually strive to inspire and love others as you do!

Karen Bell, one of my bestie's, for her support, love and beautiful painting she contributed to the cover of this book. You always know what to say and do to keep my vibration high!

In complete love and light to Blake Navarre for being the financial and emotional supporter, and my biggest fan, I thank you. Without you, I never would have had the means to move forward!

Lots of special hugs and kisses to Danyell, Marc, and Breeana Palmer and Mitchel and Carter Navarre for being the light in the center of my life and for showing up when I least expected you to. My life would have never been so full and so fun! Thanks for being the example of how to play nicely and love unconditionally!

Special acknowledgement to you, the reader of this amazing book you are about to explore, may "your days be merrier and bright" for without your interest and desire to have more fun, this book would only be pieces of paper with ink on them. I appreciate you more than words can say!

DISCLAIMER

The author of this book does not dispense medical advice or prescribe the use of any technique as a form of treatment for physical or medical problems without the advice of a physician, either directly or indirectly. The intent of the author is only to offer information of a general nature to help you in your quest for emotional and spiritual well-being. If you use the information herein for yourself, the author and the publisher assume no responsibility for your actions or the resulting outcome(s).

INTRODUCTION:
REMEMBERING TO PLAY

I play under the big bright sun; it kisses my nose and warms my soul.
I dance under the stars that sparkle like diamonds
and under the mysterious full moon light,
Any time of the day or night, it is your time to come out to play!
— Darlene Navarre

The "Go Play!" Movement

When I started talking about the idea of "playing" for adults to relieve stress and create a fun, happy, healthy life, many people just didn't understand. I realize that the idea of play generally brings up thoughts of something only children do, or something adults do in the bedroom. Many people voiced the reaction, "Play?! What are you talking about? Adults aren't supposed to play. They are supposed to work hard, make a living, retire at some point in their elder years — if they're lucky — and die." This hard road leaves most of us feeling stressed out and anything but happy.

Years ago when I was in elementary school, I was first introduced to Martin Luther King Jr.'s "I have a dream!" speech. I understood his words instinctively, because there was something inside me that wanted to inspire others to live their lives with passion and purpose, to dream big, make a positive difference in the world and, of course, have fun along the way.

It has taken me 25 years to really understand what it means to have a dream so focused and full of passion and love that I don't care how much time I spend on it because it is so fun and exciting to be a part of something bigger than myself! When I witness grown-ups having fun, uncovering new playful ways to live their life and ultimately releasing stress and worry, I feel as if I am living my dream, my purpose.

This play book was written especially for you, and not because you need another book to read or the world needs another book. This book was created to offer you a new set of rules or guidelines to live your life easily, have fun and feel good from the inside out. The reality of life is that negative contrast is going to happen. Although we prefer the bad experiences not to happen, they will, and why wouldn't we want them to? After all, experiences of pain — whether physical or emotional — allow us to more fully know what joy and health feel like. You crave more feel-good experiences the more you experience the not-so-feel-good moments. You intuitively know that within each moment of life there are amazing opportunities just waiting to be experienced.

Adding play in one area of your life, whether it is with money or in your relationship, will set you on a path of releasing stress, letting go and allowing your life to become more joyful in all areas.

I have personally found that neither exercise, food, a person nor any external thing can create our personal health and happiness. In 2003, I experienced a major shift when a stressful and contrasting situation came into my life — the most heart-breaking I have experienced to this day. It created an opportunity for me to change my thinking and create a new way to live my life. I will forever appreciate the experience Carter, my fifth and final child, gave me when he was only nine months old.

At the time, we had never given Carter anything but love, attention and breast milk during the course of those first nine months. He had never had a drug, pill or vaccination of any kind. So when my husband and I took him into the hospital, we were both very fearful, as our baby's skin was turning blue. The hospital, of course, reacted in the same manner and within seconds, he was injected with all kinds of drugs and hooked up to monitors for the first time in his life.

Within moments, the hospital staff let us know that they were not equipped to handle a baby this sick and they would be transferring him to the children's medical center by helicopter. I became more and more fearful that my son would die. While he was taken to this special hospital twenty miles away in the helicopter, my husband and I had to drive in our vehicle to meet him there.

My complete breakdown, or rather breakthrough, came the moment we arrived at the children's hospital. I was met by the emergency doctor in charge. Even though all the doctor said was, "your baby is very, very sick," I could sense his feelings of fear and sadness about my son's possible demise and unlikely recovery. After our conversation, I felt weak, as if I could hardly stand up. My fear was so strong that it took over my whole body and all I could do was sit down and cry.

This rest of this story is revealed in Chapter 11. I wanted to share this experience with you to let you know that everyone, including myself, has situations and moments of complete powerlessness, fear and stress and yet we all have the ability and power to shift these situations from bad to good.

My experience with Carter, my sweet nine-month-old baby boy, in the hospital on his "death" bed, allowed me to practice the shift in the "worst" of circumstances and you also have the opportunity — the choice — to shift your life in any circumstance as well. Focusing on what you do want, rather than what you don't, will create magic right before your eyes.

Play may be only one way to shift your thoughts and your vibration, but what better way to live the life of your dreams, feel good and have fun? So I invite you to come along, open up your heart, release your playful spirit — stop and **Go Play!**

1

WHY IS PLAY THE NEW WAY?

Why Play!
Play is Oneness…
Inspiration, Bliss,
Connection to Everything!

What Can Play Do?

Each one of us wants to feel loved, connected, important, and most of all, to feel a part of something bigger than ourselves. We all want to wake up in the morning happy just to be alive and looking forward to every moment of our day and every moment of our lives. Happiness comes from the inside out, and when we can achieve this level of self-love, the world around becomes limitless.

When you feel a complete connection to yourself, or your inner being, you naturally attract the abundance in all things. The perfect relationship, friendships, money and career will easily flow into your life — not because you worked hard for them, but simply because you learned to feel good from within. You don't need anything or anyone to "make" you happy.

I have a vision of a world in which people play their way through life. Through play, we easily connect with others, understand ourselves more, and build fun, connected, and lasting relationships. In playful environments, we create a culture of Oneness in which each player is just as important as any other. Play allows us to open up, release stress easily, and ignite the creativity and inspiration within us.

We grow, expand and dream within an environment of both positive and negative contrast, but through play, we can turn our attention towards what we truly want and create a new reality *now*. Using play and games, we can release re-sistance, pain and fear, turning them into understanding, knowing and joy! Play unites us as a whole, giving us the opportunity to accept everyone just the way they are. Your life is supposed to be easy, fun and playful! As you choose and practice playing, you will find your life unfolding in a whole new, better-than-expected way.

The Game of Life

Remember, or imagine if you can, back to when you were a wee little person just learning your way around in the world — back when you were allowed to play to learn and play to grow. Through play, you easily learned to sit up, crawl, walk, and a million other things by hearing, touching, feeling, tasting, smelling and playing.

A while later, as you began to grow up, your parents may have thought it appropriate to fill you in on **The Game of Life.** Imagine them handing you a large square box, and on the top of the box in bright bold lettering are the words "The Game of Life." Eagerly you opened the lid; you were so excited to play! You pulled out the Rule Book and all the other pieces one by one. Then, because you still struggled a bit with reading your parents offered to read the rules to you.

However, they didn't even bother to read them — they insisted that they knew the rules by heart. They began telling them to you:

The Old Rules:

Life is hard!
You will have to work hard in school and do what you're told. If you do this, you can go to college and get a good paying job.
Relationships are going to be hard work.
Having and raising children is hard work, too.
Now it's time to grow up and *stop playing around!*
Sound familiar?
Now, let's read The New Rules, given to you before you

came into your physical body. The New Rules may sound familiar because somewhere deep inside you, you have always known them. You may even be one of few people who have heard the new or rather *real* rules and are already living them. For those of you unfamiliar with the new rules, you have the opportunity for a playful shift in your life.

The New Rules:

Life is easy, fun and playful!
Happiness comes from inside you. Simply connect to your inner being through play!
You may experience contrast and negative emotions. You can easily turn your attention towards what feels good by playing!
Abundance in everything easily flows into your life, because when you feel good and you're having fun, life just gets better and better!
You are worthy, perfect and whole *now*. Anytime you want to change the direction of your life, just focus on thoughts that feel good/expansive — play and allow it all in!
Life is a fun game, so just play it!

Why is Play the New Way?

We have a human and spiritual need to thrive, grow, learn, and expand. We all have the opportunity to experience life with all its contrasting moments along the way. Once the contrast does arise, growth and expansion can come quickly as long as we turn our attention towards what feels good to us, what we really do want, and as long as we feel powerful in doing so. Play allows us to keep our attention focused on what is wanted, and then our life flows. We gain more understanding, expansion, fun and light-heartedness, rather than feeling pain and separation from our inner being.

From this space of inner connection, inspiration will flow through us and we will naturally inspire others as well. Think about the last time you had a great belly-laugh with others. I bet you inspired them to laugh simply by your laughter or perhaps their laughter inspired you. When we are inspired, we are *in-spirit* and the world around us seems brighter; more amazing situations, people and things show up for us without any effort.

One of the greatest gifts I have experienced is the birthing and upbringing of five amazing children. Over the past 23 years, I have witnessed daily miracles, all under my own roof. I've found it fascinating to watch as my children freely, playfully learned to walk, talk, climb, draw, count, and read. You name it! Small children don't think about how or why they do something; they just do it, playfully. We are all natural-born **players**!

Life is constantly in playful motion with children. Their perspective is fresh and new — they see things in the most fascinating ways. They are curious about life and thirsty to know more, to have more and to be more. Innately children are loving and give of themselves no matter what. They say what they think and they believe they are worthy and limitless!

Unconditional Love by Mitchel

Just recently, I began to enjoy running so completely that I started running five to six days a week. I love these runs because I am in nature, enjoying myself, free and flowing. I listen to books and often I come up with playful inspirations, like much of the content and ideas in this book. Running feeds my soul and allows me to clear my thoughts and start from ground zero.

On one of my long runs, I was playing around with the concept of **unconditional love**. I started to question and search for the meaning of unconditional love from my perspective and how I could better practice it. My idea of unconditional love is to love another and stay connected to my inner being no matter what is going on around me. If I saw something I did not like or saw someone doing something I found uncomfortable, I would take complete responsibility for each person or situation that showed up in my experience

and love it. I had a new commitment to practice unconditional love and to create more loving experiences in my life!

After my run, I came home to fix breakfast for my sons,
Mitchel (11) and Carter (9), their morning breakfast. While in
the middle of placing the ingredients in the blender for their
smoothie, my son Mitchel came up to me, threw his arms
around me, looked into my eyes and said, "Mom, I love you!
Do you know much I love you?"

I said in response, "No, how much?"

"Unconditionally!"

A mere ten minutes before this experience with Mitchel
was the first time I had really contemplated the idea, and I
had never spoken of this "unconditional love" concept in our
house. This shocked me, brought joy to my heart and excited me all at the same time — shocked me because I had
just finished thinking about it, filled my heart with joy as I felt
my son's love for me, and I felt excited that the Universe was
reaffirming what I was thinking and feeling.

I asked my son where he had heard about the concept
of unconditional love, and he said he didn't know. He added
"it just came to me." I was already practicing unconditional
love by creating the world around me. My son felt his complete connection to himself, towards me and wanted to share
it with me. I then asked him what he thought unconditional
love meant and he shared his thoughts. "It means no matter
what, I will always love you. I love you more than anything in
the world and I will love you forever."

I know I gain more by being the mother of these amazing
children than they may from me. Only when I brought forth
children into my life did I start to understand myself more,
and I continue to learn more about myself every day. They
are my biggest inspiration for playing through life. Because
of these five individual spirits, I started to question the world
around me and observe it from a whole new perspective. I
wanted more for myself and for them, in large part because
of my love for them.

I began to relate more to myself and understand that I

was an infinite child-like person. In the past and at times in the present, others have told me that I was crazy, weird, and needed to "grow up" and take responsibility. Because of my playful, free-spirited nature, it is easy for me to relate to my children and allow them to be children for as long as possible. When they want to do something I don't fully agree with, I honor their decision and allow them to have their experiences. When you have children, creating a playful environment can become second nature if you allow it to be.

Kids know how to be players, and without a parent or adult in the way, they easily work through their fears, frustrations and pains and get back to playing again. I have witnessed the ability of children to play through their life and I can see the contrast within the "grown up" environment, and how it feels more difficult without the adoption of play.

The majority of us in "developed" countries seem to spend a lot of time stressing out, struggling, holding on to or ignoring our emotions, practicing unhappiness, working hard, stressing out and getting nowhere. *Why,* when we live in such an expansive, abundant era, are we allowing ourselves to get in the way of our own health and happiness?

In my search for an answer to my own health and happiness, I stumbled across a few examples of people out there still playing in their adult lives. In an attempt to be more playful, many people even pay large sums of money for the experience of watching others play at football, baseball and other sporting events. People will get into debt buying boats and taking trips — all to escape the hard world they created, to find some hope, and to feel good and play.

Play does not have to be something you go out of your way to do, get in debt over, or watch others do. Play is a part of who you are. In every situation of your life, there is an opportunity to be playful and to include play as simply a natural part of life.

Who's Playing?

Each of us looks for Joy in our life in our own way. And if you believe as I do that Joy means allowing and receiving happiness without restriction, what better means of finding Joy and having Fun than playing with your dog? They never tell anyone about some of the foolish things we do, and good thing they don't!

My dog, Sweet Pea, and I play games with each other. I get down on all fours and pretend that I am a dog who competes for her toys. We growl and tug on one end or the other to see who is going to win. We wrestle on the floor and pretend we are puppies just trying to shed some extra energy.

Later, I put dancing music on and I hold Sweet Pea in my arms and we twirl round. Other times, I sit on a stool and pretend that she is my guitar and I ing to her. I can't carry a tune, yet she looks at me adoringly and doesn't seem to mind my singing out of key. When it is time for a walk, I sometimes do a cheerleading yell "One, two, three - Sweet Pea follow me!" And off we go. But the most fun is that sometimes she looks at me as another dog and other times, I see her as another person!

Joan Peck

Look at where the eyes, the attention, the dollars, the joy and the inspiration go — to the players. Of course, neither money, success, relationships, things, nor any person can "make" you happy, but aren't those things great, too? How many of us have bought into the idea "you can't have your cake and eat it too!" To that I say, "What is the point of having the cake if you can't eat it too?"

You can have it all! You deserve to have all the cake you want, and the only price to pay is that you must believe that you can have it all! When you believe in yourself and in the power within you to create the environment you want, it will all happen. Everything from happiness, wealth, success, amazing relationships and friendships will easily flow — or perhaps flood! — into your experience. Take a look around. There are plenty of people showing us that play is the way, but for most of us, it's a concept we haven't grasped in our adult life yet.

Look at those with the most wealth, freedom and happiness. These individuals, consciously or unconsciously, understand that play is the way to success and abundance in all areas. Those we look to for advice, whether it is in business, fashion or entertainment, are playing through their lives. These "players" are athletes, actors, musicians, those that play with money to create successful businesses, and those that create all the gadgets and fun things that we all enjoy.

Years ago, I remember reading a book about Donald Trump, and he said, "I love what I do so much I never need or want to take a vacation." He lives his life every day doing what he loves and loving what he is doing. Whether or not you find Donald Trump to be an icon of happiness, I will tell you this without even personally knowing him: this man is playing. More than ever, you can look at successful people and know that they understand first, how to play, and second, how to inspire others by their play.

Once you view your life as a game and you as the main player in your world, your life will start to take on a whole new light. Playing opens you up to win-win living; every situation is an opportunity to play and every person you meet is a player. Life becomes light and free, judgments of others are released, and the more you participate in the fun of your game, the more your life will flow.

Make a clear intention or decision that *play* is your new way to live, grow and be. Intend in every way and every day to be more child-like and play around with your life. Now that you have made this decision and commitment to yourself to be young and playful, regardless of your birth age, everything in your life will naturally become playful.

It is much easier to create your life from the inside out

with playful thoughts and feelings. Now is the time to know, believe and understand that you are a playful being behind all the stress and unhappiness. You were born with a creative imagination and easily played through the first few years of your life. The fact that you are a "grown-up" only means your play changes. It doesn't need to stop.

You don't need to grow up and "act your age." You can act any way you want, be anything you want and have everything. Play starts with a simple shift and adoption of a playful attitude! Upon waking each day, as you dress yourself, slip on your playful attitude, too. Look in the mirror and see the playful-spirited person you are and say, "I love me and I deserve a fun life! In every moment of today, I will find a way to play!" Move through your day being aware of your opportunities to include play.

Your stress and unhappiness can shift if you will only allow yourself to release the free, fun spirit within you. Imagine if you just took a "Go Play Stop" once a day — how different would your life be? You would be more productive in your career, your business would soar, your family and relationships would be more fulfilling and you would feel so happy just to be alive and so happy to wake up each day looking forward to the next playful opportunity coming your way. Through this simple practice, you will create a complete life of fun and abundance in all things.

Playful Presence

Play is *presence*; they are the same. Let go. Being here and now is the only place you can really be. Inspiration flows from presence and presence is the deep, true connection to yourself, your inner being, to Source (God), and other people.

Whenever you veer off track and begin thinking in terms of "have to, should, must," schedules or plans, you lose the spontaneity of inspiration, of your connection to spirit and of your true purpose, nature and playfulness. You forget how to play or what to play because you live in a world that feels stressful and hopeless. When you don't play, you stop wanting to thrive, live and expand. My husband Blake said it best when he texted to me "stop play and you might as well be dead."

I believe in you and know you deserve to play every day in every way. I know that you are a part of me and of the Source within us all. Reading this book came to you at the perfect time in the perfect place in your life. Throughout this book are Go Play Stops, stories, games and inspirations to offer you a new perspective on playing through your life.

I wrote this book especially for you — not because you needed it, but because you were asking for it. We are all asking for permission to let go, to release resistance and have fun allowing all that we truly desire in. The game is simple and the number one rule is this: "you came here, to this time/space reality, to have fun, expand and play!"

Nothing you have done is wrong, only right. The place you stand in today will be different tomorrow or even seconds from now, if you will only allow it to be different. Yes, there will be negative contrast and stressful situations from time to time along your physical path but that is why you came here. If everything were always perfectly fun and playful, you would not have the opportunity for growth and expansion. You chose to be a part of this amazing world, full of positive and (at times) negative, contrasting experiences. You wanted the perspective of the person you came to be and you will always want more.

You can always change the game, in as many ways as you like. You create the characters that come forth into your game and they will be a part of your game in the form you want. The experiences and situations in your game are your creation as well. There are so many fun and interesting variables! One thing is for certain: your thoughts and feelings build the game piece by piece, player by player, and experience by experience.

When you adopt *play as the new way* to live your life you will:

Laugh more
Smile more
Feel more blissful
Live a fuller life
Stay more connected to your inner being
Release resistance and stress
Allow more abundance to flow easily to you
Be inspired
Live in the moment
Realize your dreams.

Open up, let go and start to play your game of life the way you want it because **play can be your new way.**

2

IN THE LAND OF MAKE BELIEVE... ALL DREAMS DO COME TRUE!

Why Play!
With a playful imagination,
you grow, learn, dream and create effortlessly.

Play and Your Imagination

The imagination allows us to form pictures, images and experiences that have already happened, are happening or have not happened yet and turn them into our own personal reality. Our imagination can create images that bring emotional wellness or discord. Inside our imagination, we can create works of art or write fanciful fictional stories. Imagination is personal and through it, we each see the world from our individual point of view.

Whatever we imagine, when amplified by the emotional element, will be created in our reality whether we want it to or not. All life begins, expands and continues through the window of our imagination. Why not use your imagination to create the playful world you do want to live in, and not one you don't want?

Opening up Your Imagination

Just imagine what you could accomplish if only you use your imagination to your advantage. Napoleon Hill said, "Whatever the mind can conceive and believe, it can achieve." This concept is so completely amazing once you get the hang of using your imagination to, first, come up with fun thoughts, images and ideas, and then believe these thoughts can come true.

I have a complete fascination with movies, especially movies with amazing special effects and design, like *Avatar.* Often times, I will buy the whole package DVD set, just so I can get the special effects DVD to see how they came up with the ideas for the effects. All those amazing special effects came from moments of inspiration from within the imagination of one, or perhaps many.

Think of your imagination as your own personal art studio, where you get to create a new masterpiece with each thought. In your imagination studio, you are open and free and there are zero limits. By believing in the visions and inspirations you receive, they can easily come forth into your physical reality.

Whenever you want to consciously create, spend time in your imagination studio creating what or who you wish to show up in your life. If you find yourself unhappy with the circumstances and conditions of your life, you may want to start in your imagination studio consciously creating a new life on purpose. Creating a conscious imagination studio is much like building and decorating a brand new house.

Go Play Stop ~ Your Imagination Studio — Create Your Life in 15 Minutes a Day

Create a quiet space to relax and focus. Remember, you have zero limits — an unlimited supply of money and possibilities to build your perfect imagination studio. First, think of the perfect location to build your studio. Is it on the beaches of Hawaii surrounded by the sounds of the ocean or in the forest with big tall trees and birds chirping away? Next what does your studio look like? What are its shape, lighting, and texture? Once it is built, you need to collect the key that is magically placed in your heart. Place your hand over your heart, open it up and begin to decorate your studio, your life, with the thoughts and feelings you would like your life to be.

Keep the inside of this magical space of your imagination studio clear and free by clearing away any negative thoughts or beliefs you may be storing inside your mind. You can simply and easily release these thoughts and past images that are no longer serving you by focusing on what those thoughts have caused you to *want* instead, for example "I want more money!" Then, paint the picture of what "more money" looks like. You can also support yourself by releasing negative thoughts altogether. Every morning you can look in the mirror and say "Today, I start over fresh, with new creative thoughts of the life I DO want to create!"

What is really important to understand about your life and your imagination is that *you* are the complete creator of your reality. This includes everything you see, hear, and experience in others and the life around you. Everything in your life is your responsibility! Accept this responsibility from a space of complete love and power, not from the space of blame.

Before you get all wild and creative, simply sit for a minute, and take a few deep breaths, feeling the expansiveness, possibilities and life force flowing within this space where your mind, emotions and inspiration meet. Begin to imagine your highest, innermost being, awaiting you in your studio and connect with it. Here in this creative space, your life is always fresh and new. In this space, ideas and inspiration flow in with ease. Any time you are not satisfied with your reality, come back to a neutral space, take some deep breaths and reconnect again to what you do want with intensity and passion.

Now that you are centered, pull out your paints, your computer design program, put on your dancing shoes, or use any artistic modality or creative avenue of your choice. Take a moment to imagine yourself playing in your creative art studio. Imagine you have merged with your inner being/higher self and with Source (God) and they support you and give you exactly what you want to create. This is your very own private space to create. Only you can invite new ideas, thoughts and the people you wish to paint, sculpt, program or dance with into your life experience.

You get to play around, laugh, be, do and have anything here without any judgment, pain or interruptions. Imagine yourself opening your heart to anything that is fun, creative, playful and inspiring. You feel safe, secure and peaceful; you are confident and there is complete knowing and under-standing of all things within this space. You can ask questions here and answers quickly flow in. You are ready to cre-ate — free your playful spirit, and make this new imagination studio a part of your everyday life!

Throughout the day, remember to practice thinking thoughts and imagining things (and people), whether "real" or not, that excite you or cause you to feel good. The more you imagine the possibilities of your future with clear inten-sity and a "burning desire," the more these possibilities will become a reality.

Go Play Stop ~ Imagine Your Playful Life One Area at a Time

When your imagination is clear and you are open to receiving and creating, it is time to imagine the playful life you wish to create. Of course, if you are already seeing and imagining parts of your life you are enjoying, then by all means, continue to allow those to flow.

Leading from our imagination, inspiration, heart, and positive emotions allows us to connect with what feels good and true to us rather than following logic or the guidance of others and finding ourselves feeling uncertain, powerless and lost.

There are five main areas of our lives that affect our reality:
- Personal relationships
- Friendships
- Career or business
- Financial abundance
- Your center: body, mind, and spirit.

Each of these areas affects the others, but if you focus on one area, the rest usually come into balance if you allow them to. Of course, the opposite is true as well; if you are focused on the "reality" of a current health concern, your career might begin to go badly. Next, it may affect your personal relationship, such as finding yourself often fighting with your mate. Even the car you drive may start breaking down and the next thing you know, your finances decrease.

One Playful Thought Closer: When you look at all the areas of your life and feel overwhelmed by everything that is going on, take a step back and a few deep breaths, too. The key is to not look at the whole picture, just yet — focus only on one area in your life you can feel good about and focus on that part only. Then, you may break down one problem or challenge into small pieces. This allows you to easily become playful in one area of your life. Before you know it, everything in your life comes into playful alignment.

Take one of the five areas of life listed above where you can see some kind of hope or that feels better than the others and build from that thought. For example, if you believe that you and your mate are great together but your arguing is really over silly stuff, you can start with your personal relationship.

Get focused and clear about new playful ideas you can create with your partner. Make a list of things you can personally do to create more fun and play in your life. Focus strongly on — even *obsess* over — all your beautiful ideas, thoughts and emotions — anything that feels good towards your mate. You must do this until you have a burning desire to create more love and play surrounding your relationship. You will find that if you practice this playful process consistently, you will create a great deal of joy in your relationship and ultimately in all areas of your life as well.

Throughout the rest of this book, there are more inspirations and playful processes to try in every part of your life. In order to jumpstart your playful muscles, I find it important to get your imagination primed and pumped up first, because

your thoughts and emotions are central to your playful experiences. You can eagerly anticipate and set in motion the
idea of play and open your imagination to playing as a way
of being.

Imagine Playful Loving Relationships and Friendships

I wonder, if we were programmed throughout our lives
that relationships are easy, men understood women and
women understood men, how different our world would be.
Instead, we are told the opposite — that marriage and intimate relationships are hard. Rather than focusing on the
problems in your relationship, or the lack of one, think of the
idea that you created this experience to expand your understanding from and you're ready to release the past experiences that no longer support you and start fresh. There is
really no need to understand the why and how of what is not
going "right" — instead, try to see the mirror within your relationships and your part in it.

We are all mirrors of one another; what we see in another that we do not like is only a belief we have within ourselves, and we have the opportunity to release it. If you do
not currently have an intimate relationship (whether you want
one or not), this is also a mirror for you. You can grow, expand and know yourself more within all relationships. Look
into your past experiences from the mirror perspective. Release any resistance — thoughts and feelings of what you do
not want. This allows you to open up for new experiences
you do wish to have.

If a relationship "problem" or "issue" you are currently
experiencing with another person, or one from the past,
comes up in your thoughts and you feel strong negative
emotions from it, you can release it forever. While thinking of
the memory, tell yourself, "This is my responsibility. I brought
this person (or situation) into my experience." By taking responsibility for your situation or the people you invited into
your reality, you are empowered to do something about it,

rather than taking the victim role which is very disempowering. From empowerment, you have the ability to change your thoughts around the subject as well as any present or future experiences.

When emotions come up that I don't really want to experience, I start by first appreciating the situation and the person (or people) involved. By feeling appreciation, I immediately begin to feel better and more empowered to release the situation altogether. It also helps to remember this experience is a gift, because it has led me to know more about what I do want, and allowed me to know myself more as well.

The feeling of appreciation encompasses love and enables you to attract experiences you want. Unwanted experiences are bits of contrast allowing us to learn, grow and expand. Contrast is all part of the fun of living in this time/space reality. By releasing the negative memories within your imagination surrounding your relationships, you generate space to create the playful relationships you are ready and wanting to have.

You are free to focus on what you do want in your current relationship or for a new relationship to flow forth. If you still are not clear about the person or people you would enjoy coming into your reality, there is playful process in Chapter 6 for creating the relationship of your dreams. For the moment, you have shifted your focus and will begin receiving inspiration.

It's time to imagine your new relationship into reality! You can even open yourself up to inspiration by saying to yourself, "Universe (or your higher power), I am open to receiving inspiration of a playful, loving relationship!" Now, as you go about your day feeling happy just to be alive, pay attention to the inspiration the Universe is sending you about a new playful, loving relationship.

Imagining Your Perfect Career

Whether you have a career, job or business, it is most

important for your well-being for you to love what you do. Doing what you love can be one of the most fulfilling parts of your life. We naturally want to do things that inspire us, and to be a part of inspiring others.

When you have settled for a career, job or business that is not a source of inspiration and enjoyment to you, and does not utilize your gifts and talents, it is time for a change. You can only do something uninspiring for so long before you may begin to experience a breakdown in other areas of your life — your health, relationships or financial abundance.

I was raised by a father who disliked his job, and he worked at that uninspiring job for 25 years. The stress of feeling trapped and not doing what he loved took a toll on his health. He suffered with stomach pains for about 25 years (coincidence?) and passed on at only 50 years old.

My dad knew what he loved and what he was passionate about — computers — but he choose not to believe, or imagine, that he could create wealth from it. Out of obligation to support his family, he gave up and gave in to what he did not want to do. Does it have to be this way? Do we have to give up a love of something because of our past choices and obligations? Men and women who feel trapped like my dad did have several options, including using their imagination and dreaming a better career or business into reality.

The truth is that all comes down to your imagination — focus and believe that you can do what you love to do. Continuing to imagine yourself doing what you love and continuing to focus on that thought is all you really need to do. *How* it will happen is the Universe's job. Life can be — and is — that easy.

Imagine Abundance

If you could understand but one thing to support you in changing your financial circumstances it is this: there is abundance in all things! Years ago, I heard a story about a late 1800's preacher who traveled by horse all around the United States preaching to young adults and teenagers about abundance. His message was clear, "God wants you to be rich!" Just look around you and you will see how abundant nature and the whole world is.

I find it interesting to hear or read about people who believe that if the rich have most of the wealth, this leaves less for others. Abundance is as expansive as our imaginations if we believe in the abundance of all things. Is it really true that if I have something, like money, then I am taking from and leaving less for others? That is much like saying "Will you please breathe less, so there will be enough oxygen for me." Think, feel and imagine the expansion and abundance first, and then the Universe will bring you what you are a match for.

Again, as with anything, when you can imagine abundance — or wealth, health or your perfect passionate career — as if it already exists, the Universe must bring it into your reality. There is nothing you must learn or do in order to allow wealth and abundance in all things, except feel the feelings and think the thoughts of what it is you want.

Everything is yours to have, be, and do! The Universe is saying "YES" to everything you want; it is only your current beliefs that are keeping your abundance away. It takes no more energy to manifest a million dollars than it does a penny — it is only your thoughts and beliefs that are not allowing the million dollars to easily flow into your bank account. I promise you, it is your birthright to be wealthy and abundant in all things! With your imagination, you can change your beliefs and thoughts surrounding wealth and money; then simply allow it to easily flow to you!

Imagine Your Center: Body, Mind and Spirit

For years, it has been my passion to be healthy and inspire others to be healthy as well. I have spent more of my life researching health, food and personal growth than almost anything else. I believe it all started at a young age when I experienced illness myself and witnessed my father's pain as well.

These days, I feel healthier and more in balance when I enjoy fresh, whole, raw fruits and vegetables, but at the same time, I have found that health is created in my mind or imagination first. Your body has amazing synergy and it only responds to how you think and feel about it. Did you know that you can use your imagination to heal yourself and others as well? When we change our view of the world the world around us changes too.

I know my own weight, health, mental clarity and spiritual connection have improved because I play with my thoughts and feelings about myself, and I imagine what I want to create. Every day, I love and appreciate my body, my mind and my spirit for the life I have and for the harmonious interactions that allow me to enjoy my life more fully. There is such power in appreciation; when you are in the flow of appreciation, your imagination kicks into overdrive because when you feel good emotionally, every part of your physical being feels good, too.

I know that my fresh thoughts, feelings and actions of love and appreciation for all of my life keep me centered. I focus on connecting with myself by thinking thoughts that feel good, taking care of my body by making fresh food choices, doing physical movement (exercise), and spending time loving and appreciating myself. I consider the choice of fresh thinking, foods and movement to be the most important part of living in our physical reality. When you are centered and at peace with who you are and care about the thoughts and foods you take into your body, you will have more than enough to give to others and you will naturally inspire them as well.

Being "self centered" has allowed me to have a great figure and excellent health, to think wonderfully creative and clear ideas, and to free myself to play and be with others, loving everyone unconditionally as I love myself. Love of self breeds more love to give and receive from others. Imagine yourself each day, enjoying life and feeling healthy and happy and the Universe will make it so.

Connecting to Source and Boosting Your Imagination

Since I was very young, I have felt like I wanted do something that would positively affect others. For years, I was searching in the dark trying to find the light — my passionate purpose that would allow me to inspire others. Focusing on the thought that I was not yet leading a life of higher purpose led me into bouts of depression and sadness.

The older my children became, the more I was scared and worried that I hadn't found my higher purpose. I wondered daily, that beyond my purpose and inspiration to my children, what was I going to do? My lack of faith and my feeling of an unfulfilled mission left me angry and frustrated. I ended up taking out my anger and frustration on my husband, or by yelling at my children, until finally my husband just couldn't take it anymore.

One day I discovered that my husband was having an emotional affair with another woman and when I confronted him, he told me he no longer wanted to be with me and was no longer "in love" with me. I felt like I was living in a nightmare. It was one of the worst days of my life. What I didn't realize at the time was how the separation between us would become a rebirthing experience for myself. It led to many major personal insights from me writing this book, and to one of the most electrifying dreams I have ever had that I can still remember to this day.

From the time I was five years old, I always had a feeling of being trapped. No matter what I would do, where I would go, or what relationship I was in, I felt trapped. One morning in September 2011, I had a dream that changed the direction of my life completely.

It was like a scene from a movie, back when people wanted to publicly humiliate others they thought were wrong in some way. They would lock them in a "stock" — a contraption in which their wrists and neck were laid on top of a wooden beam with just enough room for them to fix and then another piece of wood would go on top keeping them captive or "trapped". Essentially, the person's head and hands would be exposed sticking out and the rest of their body was behind the wood.

My head was in the stock, tilted to the side, and I was sobbing, and staring at my higher, brighter self. My emotions ran deep and I could hear myself apologizing to my inner being, asking for forgiveness and almost begging for the chance to finally live up to my full potential. I felt exhausted from the way I had been thinking, feeling and reacting to situations in my life. At the time I was focused on thoughts of my dissolving marriage which were leaving me feeling powerless, jealous and insecure for the first time since I was a child.

As my inner being stood there looking at me with complete unconditional love and peace, she said to me in a soft, kind voice, "There is no lock. You can easily break free anytime you want." I started to cry harder, begging for forgiveness and again my inner being said, "There is no lock. You can free yourself anytime." After a few more times of me sobbing, her allowing and acknowledging me, I could finally hear what she was telling me. I realized that I was the one trapping myself and that I could free myself from this entrapment anytime I wanted.

I powerfully pushed myself up and out, breaking free from my contraption and stood up, straight and tall with my hands on my hips — much like a powerful superwoman pose. I felt a sense of freedom and power beyond any I had previously felt. The next thing I knew, I was moving towards my higher self and she towards me. We merged into one being, and I felt a sense of peace and power wash over me.

I felt completely new and fresh, with tingles throughout my body. I felt strong, invincible, and worthy beyond any feeling I had felt before. There was an incredible sense of peace and freedom flowing through my body.

Within moments, I woke up from my dream, feeling more amazing than I had ever felt upon waking in the past. I was free from every trap I had placed myself in. Once in a while, when any feeling of limits or entrapment comes up, I remember the dream and remind myself there is no lock except that which I create and I am free again to release myself from it.

You, too, can release yourself from the traps or chains you impose upon yourself. Imagine your freedom, your release, and it will be. Like Dorothy in the *Wizard of Oz*, you always have the knowledge and ability to go home. Perhaps it is our active imagination focusing on things we don't want or memories of the past that keep us a prisoner of our dramatic struggles of pain, sorrow, or stress over our current circumstances. We can use this same imagination to release us to experience a life of joy and play by paying attention to thoughts or memories that feel good instead. Imagine freeing yourself; remember what it felt like to be young, free, laughing and playing. Now recreate your new existence with the same feelings you once felt long ago.

Close your eyes; get into your creative studio and imagine the young, vibrant player you once were and merge your "grown-up" self with the youthful you of the past. Feel the laughter, joy and exhilaration as you are washed over with feelings of delight and playfulness. Now open your eyes and stand in front of the mirror as your new, playful self.

Look into your eyes, yet at the same time, look beyond your eyes. See deep into the renewed, fresh, and more playful you. Send unconditional love and peace deep into you. Now stand back from the mirror — tall, strong and powerful. Place your hands on your hips in super-person style and feel your renewed sense of playful youthfulness reemerge, taking over each cell of your body.

From this moment on, you are ready to accept and allow inspiration to flow through you. You have opened up your imagination and are ready to create the playful, vigorous life you came here to live. Remember, in the land of imagination, all dreams really *DO* come true!

3

PLAY TIME!

Why Play!
Playing games
releases resistance and stress…
then joy flows easily.

Grown-Up Play Dates

I love getting up in the morning and working on my current projects or accomplishing items on my ever-increasing To Do list. Even though I enjoy my work, I occasionally need to catch my breath and refuel my creative reservoir so I can continue to my bring my best self to my personal and professional commitments. I have been known to spontaneously plan a quick, one-day hiatus out of town during the middle of the week. Nothing makes me happier than playing "tourist" for the day and experiencing the sights, smells, and sounds of a new city or a local destination.

I recently booked a same-day round-trip flight to San Francisco from Las Vegas, for a quick mental break when plane tickets were extremely cheap. I left early on a Tuesday morning and returned late in the evening. I visited art galleries, took a cable car through the city, and devoured a hot-fudge sundae while sitting on a park bench watching three 80-year-old men swim in the San Francisco Bay (I am sure their endeavor was a dare).

Sometimes, I grab a friend to come and play with me on my excursions, although I love traveling solo because I have the freedom to explore my new surroundings without any timelines or worrying about anyone else's level of enjoyment. I often meet new people at the airport, restaurants, museums, or other cultural attractions, and I rarely spend a lot of money because I am running around the city on foot or utilizing public transportation to take in the sights and get around town. The best part about my grown-up play time is that I come home refreshed and inspired and I have created a new special memory that I can revisit anytime. There is no greater joy than exploring a new city or your own backyard if even for a day.

Patrice Snead

For the Play of It

I hope by this point you have an understanding of and passion for play. Your imagination is clear, the idea of play as a new way of living and being is now flowing through you, and you just can't wait to play! Right?

Perhaps, like many, your play muscles still need a bit of stretching, warming up and practice. If you would like a bit of inspiration on how or what to play, this is the perfect chapter for you. Often, due to working hard and feeling stressed out about your life, you may leave your playful spirit in the far corner of the attic of your soul. These **Go Play Stops** are meant to jog your memory and unleash your playful spirit again.

Remember, play is supposed to feel good, be fun and inspire you to want more! Play is an attitude, so put it on and let's get playing.

Go Play Stop ~ Ways to Play Like a Kid Again

Hop Scotch: Get out some chalk (or you can use a rock) and draw a hop scotch diagram on the sidewalk or driveway. If you have kids, invite them to play as well. Pretend you are five years old again and play freely. Just think, you can jump to number 10 much easier now that you're big!
Hula Hoop: You can purchase or make a hula hoop to

swing your hips around and dance to some music. To make a hula hoop: buy or find some flexible PVC pipe, a piece of plastic to connect the two ends, and electrical tape. The heavier the hoop, the easier it is to hula. The hula hoop is the right size when it comes up to your waist when you stand it upright. I had never been able to hula until I created my own hula hoop like this. I have since taken my hula hoop everywhere, and when other adults see me hula, they all what to join and play along.

Jump Rope: There are two ways to jump rope — with a single rope, and with a large rope along with others. My favorite way to jump rope is with others, but if you are all by yourself or are not ready to include others in your play, then single jump roping can be fun, too. For group jumping, just purchase rope at a hardware store and tie it or burn it at both ends. For single jumping, buy a rope from the toy section or at a fitness store. To check if the rope is the right length, stand on it with one foot and pull the ends straight up. The handles should reach to your armpits at least, and no higher than the top of your shoulder joint. If you have forgotten how to jump rope, simply swing the rope forward and back, jumping right before it hits your legs, until you start to get the hang of it again. I love to skip and jump rope — it makes me feel so child-like and gets me in a perfect playful state.

Juggle: Justin is a 29-year-young friend of mine who just learned and fell in love with juggling. He has found his passion and now even attends juggling conferences. He has so much fun and is learning all kinds of new tricks and ways to juggle. The great thing is you can juggle almost anything from a couple of pieces of fruit, tennis balls, to bowling pins or chainsaws (practice on balls and fruit first)! The point is to have fun and feel youthful again.

Play Ball: Baseball, catch, soccer, football, basketball, beach volleyball... I love it when I see adults, often men, enjoying a day of playing sports. My brother used to play football every Saturday with his wife's family and friends and loved it. Sports are not just for men women who play ball can have fun too.

Our family loves to play soccer together and sometimes we play soccer baseball — the same concept as baseball, just kicking a soccer ball instead of hitting a ball with a bat. This is great if you have younger kids — it is easier to learn to kick than it is to hit a ball with a bat. For cold days, buy balloons, blow them up, put all your breakables away and start hitting the balloons around with your hands. Playing ball is the best with loads of people, so invite the neighborhood kids and adults to play with you.

Tag, You're it: It seems the only tag we adults play is phone tag. Of course, tag may require other players and your friends may think you are crazy, so if you don't have your own children, invite your friends who do. You can inspire (and reassure) your friends by telling them you are doing a "30 Day Play Experiment" to relieve stress.

Every kid under the age of ten would love to play tag. If you go to a park where there are kids, enroll the parents by inspiring them to relieve stress through play, too. Most adults are under some kind of stress, so those without kids may be open to playing as well. Who knows, from your playful idea, you may help create a connection between the parents at the park and their children.

Ride a Bike or Roller Skate: I know, riding a bike may not seem like the most fun a kid can have, but remember kids don't just ride bikes, they play with them. Ride down a large hill as fast as you can. Ride your bike with no hands. Lift your feet off the pedals and spread them out as you ride down the street. Stand up on your bike, lean forward to your handle bars, stand up on the pedals, squeeze your legs to-gether and lift your hands up towards the sky. Exhilarating!

I love to roller skate and, believe it or not, they still sell four-wheel roller skates at sporting goods stores. You can roller skate down hills as well (please be comfortable stop-ping first). Skate as fast as you can up a hill. Just think, now you can skate as far as you like without your mom or dad telling you "no." Roller blades are great too, and both are a great way to move your body, relieve stress and have fun playing around.

Water Fight: When I was young, I remember my mom and two of the neighbor guys starting a water fight that went on for years. Just about everyone in the circle I grew up in washed their cars on Saturdays once or twice a month. One day, the neighbor gentleman and my mom were washing their cars at the same time. He, being the playful man he was, "accidentally" sprayed my mom with water.

Of course my mom, being the playful woman she was, sprayed him back. This went on for years; as more kids got involved, so did more parents. It turned into a Saturday tradition and we all had a blast! There are plenty of opportunities to take a large bucket to the park, bring large plastic cups, fill the bucket with water, and invite everyone at the park to a playfully fun water fight.

Park Time: Head over to a park and play on the playground equipment. Every time I am at the park, with or without my kids, I enjoy swinging, twirling or climbing on the playground equipment. I get plenty of looks from fellow parents but I don't care. Besides, from the looks on their faces, I think they would like to play with me — time to inspire other adults to get in the game and play, too.

Finger Paint: There are so many options for finger painting even if you don't have finger paints. I can think of many fun ingredients I could use to finger paint. Wow, this play stuff sure opens up your imagination! Finger painting foods: mash up an avocado with your hands, blend up avocado with beets or carrots, use flour mixed with water and food coloring, the possibilities are endless. Find something soft, mushy and colorful you can paint with and you have finger paints. The picture you create can be abstract or have some kind of meaning to you. Stay free, have fun and let your imagination run wild!

Go Play Stop ~ Playful Adventures

The Family Treasure Hunt

I wanted something fun for the kids as a family outing, at the time when our kids were 10, 8, and 3. This idea of a family adventure popped in my head — a Treasure Hunt. So I created a treasure map using landmarks within an area I was already familiar with.

I took a plain white piece of paper, stained it with dry, ground coffee beans and burned the edges to make it look old. Then I wrote it in similar fashion to a kids Disney adventure movie writing in the landmarks as riddles leading to a second map with more clues that led to the treasure.

The older children were skeptical at first, but as the clues mounted they could not help themselves. They were immersed in the adventure and were moving at a quickened pace to the next clue. By the time they reached the second map they could no long contain their excitement and were now running to each new clue. When they reached the final clue the treasure was buried beneath a maker.

I had told the children that it may or may not be a real treasure map but I said we could find nothing, something really scary or we may find something from an old bank robbery, in which case we would split the loot amongst all of us. In fact, I had hidden just enough money, some paper cash and some coins, to add some drama and a toy for each child. The money was the exact amount for our whole family to go to a movie that afternoon.

The Treasure Hunt was an engaging way for our family to connect and have fun together. Now as adults, one of our children's fondest memories is of that family Treasure Hunt adventure.

Blake Navarre

Get Lost: Take a trip without a navigation system and go somewhere you have never been before. Get lost, and leave it open to the Universe to match you up with an inspiring trip. Be open to discovering new places, people and things you have never seen before.

Drive from complete trust and faith in the Universe. If you see an interesting side road, take it. Go on pure instinct and not your thoughts. Just think of all the places you'll go and playful people you will meet. When you show genuine interest in another, they feel it and they in turn become interested in you.

If you get lost enough, you may find your way in life more often. Sit back, relax, drive and experience a whole new world unfolding before your eyes. When you're ready to come home, ask for directions or simply discover your way back.

Face a Fear: Get powerfully playful and face a fear. Facing fears is exhilarating and in the end it is more fun than anything you may ever do. It is the ultimate accomplishment, and when you face a fear, you are renewed. No longer does some idea have a hold on you — you become the leader in your life. Start with baby steps, climb smaller mountains first, and work your way up to bigger and grander mountains.

For years, I was afraid of heights. One year, we moved to a small town surrounded by mountains of various sizes, some right outside our back yard. I began climbing small mountains at first, a couple of times a week, then I increased to larger mountains. By the end of a month, I was able to climb to the top of the largest mountain in Boulder City, Nevada. A few months later, I was able to do a ropes course and stood atop a 78-foot telephone pole with only a harness attached to my back. Without fear, I free-fell off and did it again because it felt so good. Now, I am completely free of my fear of heights and feel empowered.

Sarah was extremely scared of public speaking. To promote a book she was writing, she wanted to face her fear of public speaking in case she ever had the opportunity to speak in front of a large audience. She started with small steps and joined a Toastmasters group. After a month of getting to know the people in the group, she was able to stand up in front of 20 people — now her friends — and speak about herself.

Over the course of a year, she pushed herself to talk at least once a month in front of her Toastmasters group. She started to become so at-ease, they asked her to speak at a conference in front of 50 people. Two years later, she was up in front of hundreds of people promoting her book.

When I asked Sarah how she was able to speak in front of hundreds of people, she did not know. She simply said "I greet them all at the door before they enter. I get to know them and now they are no longer people I don't know, they are my friends." Even though she still gets nervous before a speaking event, she is able to do it flawlessly and she feels powerful when she is doing it. Feeling powerful is fun and playful!

Spontaneous Tripping: Be spontaneous and take off for a day or a weekend. To the detriment of my children (so they tell me), my husband and I tend to be very spontaneous people. We love to just take off for a day trip on his motorcycle or go to California for the weekend. Before we had our two youngest boys, we would take off to California or Utah for days all alone, and now we get to take them along.

In a world with so many schedules, being spontaneous is playful. You can follow your heart and intuition instead of your head. Isn't it time you get out of your head and take off? If you do have children and find this more difficult, have a babysitter on back-up a couple of weekends a month. You can even leave your plans open to spontaneity and just plan to have the sitter there to support you.

Spontaneity is not limited to taking trips: out of the blue, buy a friend or loved one a gift "just because." Take yourself out to lunch. Stand up and start dancing at work or call out "I love you!" in the grocery store. Find playful ways to combine your creativity and spontaneity to have a blast.

Sky Dive: Jumping out of a plane, with a parachute, has to be one of the most exciting and crazy experiences. Some people have such a great time doing it that they do it for a playful career. Sky diving may be one of the closest things to feeling like a bird free falling from the sky to the earth. This exhilarating adventure could be the next step in facing your fear of heights. I know it is definitely on the top of my bucket list.

I have two friends, Vicki and Cheri, who wanted to launch their business and face their biggest fear all at the same time. Their idea was that if they could face their bigger fear (heights), they could face any fear they may come up against in their business. Twelve thousand feet up, as each woman was individually strapped to a professional "jumper," they sky dived out of the airplane and within minutes they safely drifted back to ground. It has been months since the launch of their business and their sky diving experience and they both tell me they are now able to easily face any fears that come their way — and they had so much fun doing it, they can't wait to do it again.

Bungee Jump: My adventurous friend, Annetta, has gone both bungee jumping and tandem sky diving. She said the experience of bungee jumping was far more thrilling. She told me free falling without anything more than a harness around her waist and through her legs was more fun and exciting than jumping out of a plane with a parachute and another person strapped to the back of her.

If you are a person who, like me, has a bold spirit and loves playful adventures like sky diving and you haven't tried bungee jumping yet, now is the time — what better way to stretch your play muscles and jump!

Ropes Course: For years I wanted to play through a ropes course, and I finally got my opportunity at a leadership training workshop. The only part I didn't like about it was the limited time I had to do it — only one afternoon. It was so adventurously fun! There were four separate challenges, from walking across a 12-foot-long log suspended up fifty feet to the 78-foot-tall telephone pole free fall jump.

I walked across two tightrope wires positioned side by side and then a single wire — both without nets and with only a simple harness attached to my back. A ropes course is perfect for those who are looking for a safe, playful, heights adventure.

Motorcycle Fun: My husband's favorite adventure is anything using motorcycles. From dirt bikes to road bikes, motorcycles release his worries and free his playful spirit. Back when we met, one of the deep connections we had was our love of motorcycle adventures. Our shared affinity for motorcycles began back when we were both very young.

My mother shared this story with anyone that would listen: I am the eldest of four children, and when I was born, my mom and dad didn't know what to do for a baby who would not stop crying. My parents, being the creative couple they were, decided to try motorcycle riding with me.

Of course, this was on a quiet, residential road and not necessarily something I am advocating in this book. With my dad driving the motorcycle, my mom behind him, they would place me in between them and ride up and down the street. This put me to sleep and they survived the crying baby moments and felt relief from the ride as well.

My parents found a creative way to play with their baby and calm her down at the same time. To this day, I love motorcycles and can't wait to get my motorcycle license now that my five children are older. If you don't have a motorcycle, rent one for a day and create a playful adventure with the wind flowing around you... pure freedom!

Roller Coaster Riding: One of my favorite adventures as a kid was visiting our local amusement park. Even though I was only able to visit two times a year, it is still one of my fondest memories of childhood. I remember when my friends and I would ride the roller coaster over and over again. When we finished one ride we would race to get in line again. We rode every ride in the park and some, like the roller coaster, four times at least.

Now, I live in Las Vegas, and even though I have been on the New York, New York roller coaster a few times, I long to attend another amusement park and ride a roller coaster over and over again. I have read about people who travel around riding roller coasters in various places and amusement parks. Adventures happen for those that seize the moment and create it in their experience. Are you ready for some roller coaster fun?

Drive Fast: How many of us have had a speeding ticket in the past? Most of us love to drive fast and we would most likely drive faster if we could get away with it, despite the risks. I, personally, am a little afraid to own a sports car. Don't get me wrong — I love sports cars! However, I can't help but think "what is the point of all that speed and power when I can't take it to the limit?"

An alternative to paying speeding tickets or other reckless driving charges is to visit a race track and rent a race car for a couple of hours. Imagine how much fun it would be to drive as fast as you can. You can use your imagination and race around the track, imagining you are an official Nascar driver. I have several friends who have done this and they all say it is one of the most fun things they have ever done.

Canoeing, Kayaking or Boating: Teresa is the owner of Flow North Paddling Company. For your playful, adventurous enjoyment, her company rents out canoes and kayaks for the day. Teresa takes herself on fun expeditions canoeing on various rivers in Canada. Floating and paddling on the water is her play.

The water can be so calm and serene, and paddling can be very meditative. On some rivers, it's calm and relaxing until you round a bend and find rapids and waves of adventure and excitement. Nature provides us with an amazing playground where we can play, relax, or get excited. From the water to the forests, seek out playful adventures wherever you are inspired to explore.

Go Play Stop ~ Lazy Day Plays

People Watch: I have such an active imagination that I love to people watch and make up creative stories. I love to travel and traveling with five children has given me plenty of opportunities to come up with distracting playful games. As the kids and I travel back and forth in the car to various places on road trips, we play the "What's Your Story" game for fun.

In the "What's Your Story" game, as we see people walking, biking or riding in their vehicles, we start to make up their story from our perspective. Even when you are in conversation with another, and he is telling you a story about his life, you still essentially make it up in your mind. You filter the information you receive from him based on your previous memories. In this game, you are simply making up the information altogether, without any input from the other person.

For example, driving around our town of Boulder City, Nevada, we might pass by a young woman running fast and free. I might start the game by telling a story about what she does; she's a college student at the University of Nevada and she runs to clear her mind. My daughter might add "she has a boyfriend she is deeply in love with, and they are both going to be artists." My son may add "Yeah, her boyfriend wants to marry her and is going to ask her after he makes her dinner. They are going to live together first and get married on the beach after he wins a surfing contest."

Basically, we make a version of this woman's life we really know nothing about, but it is just fun and creative to make up our version of her happily ever after. You can play this game anytime and anywhere. A friend and I love to just watch people living out their lives in front of us. We watch how they dance and admire their style, or witness the way they interact with one another while in a group. The point of the game is to relax, sit back, and be in the moment witness-ing those around you playing.

Fun Moments: How often do you spend time focused on living your life in the very moment it is happening? Without previous thoughts or judgment, there is a playful possibility in every moment in every situation throughout your day. Wash-ing the car with your lover can turn into water play. Even vacuuming the floor can be playful when you hook up the hose and all of a sudden you become a suction monster. My kids love it when I play around with the hose, pretending to suck them or a large ball up.

Pay attention and become playfully aware that your life is unfolding in ways you were not "present to" before. Notice things you have never seen before; see yourself, others and life in new, inspired moments.

Photography Fun: On Apple computers there is a program named Photo Booth that is able to take pictures in fun and playful ways. When my friend, Dixie, received her new Mac computer, she and I opened up the program and started creating alien-looking figures of ourselves. We laughed and played with this for a couple of hours.

If taking pictures feels playful to you, go out and record the world around you through photography. You can play with the colors, composition and distortion, creating works of art and magic. Today, there are various apps for smart phones that will allow you to make the world look new and fun through the creative lens of your phone. If you're so in-clined, photography can give you loads of fun and play for a day.

Day at a Spa: If you are like many over-worked and under-played men and women, a relaxing day at the spa, or in your own spa, is all the play you need to rejuvenate your spirit. If your budget doesn't quite allow for you to attend a fancy spa, then simply create your own.

Make sure the kids, dog and others around you know you are taking a "play out" and need to be left alone to re-charge your spirit. Have your favorite music in the background, light candles around a hot bubble bath, or light some incense. Step into your bath and step into your escape... lay back and imagine you are in a spa. Relax, unwind and release all your troubles, problems and worries, allowing them to melt away. When you drain the bath water all of the "stuff" that you were carrying around drains, too. You are left to play the rest of the day!

Cleaning and Organizing: I find it amazing how we are able to do something like clean our closet out and feel physically and emotionally clearer. I even read about a psychiatrist who would recommend her patients clean out their dresser drawers when they had a problem plaguing their life. The patients would come back and report feeling better, and if they still had more emotions to release, she would ask them to clean their closet. Eventually their worries would be cleaned and organized away. If you clean and organize in a playful way, you optimize the emotional release you feel.

Years ago, Grace called me up and was feeling stressed over doing the dishes. Originally, her husband and she had made an arrangement that she would do all the cooking and he would do the dishes. This was working great for both of them, that is until he started working so many hours he was no longer able to attend to the dishes on a weekly basis. She was upset because her kitchen was a mess and it was becoming too difficult to cook when most of the dishes were piling up. They didn't have a dishwasher, so I asked her if she would be willing to do the dishes herself if it was fun. She asked me how:

1. Clear all the dishes out of the sink and fill the sink up with clean hot water and lots of bubbles — so much so that the bubbles are overflowing above the water. Who doesn't just love bubbles?
2. A scrubber that feels good in your hand is very important, and it can be colorful too! A great scrubber can also become your microphone (hint, hint).
3. Rub your favorite lotion on your hands and then cover them with tall plastic gloves. Might as well pamper your

hands while you dish.
4. Turn on your favorite music — something that really feels good! Music can be an amazing element to any cleaning or organizing activity.
5. Now, it's time to shake your "booty", blow around some bubbles, sing along and play with the dishes.

This small, playful activity changed Grace's perspective and attitude on dishes and to this day, she loves dish time. You can add the element of play into any activity throughout your day.

Another way to spread the love and playful way is to be of service to others. Feel free to take an hour of your time on a lazy afternoon and sweep off a neighbor's front porch or mow their lawn. Bring some music along and make it a joyous experience. A few years ago, when a friend's four little girls were quite small, we used to get together once a week for love, fun and support. While there, we would spend an hour just folding clothes. Her life was extremely busy and the laundry would end up piled on the couch. She and I had the most joyous time talking, listening, folding laundry and connecting — in the end, we both felt amazing and the house was clean. Giving to others can be fun, playful and fill up your heart and soul.

Cartoon Screenwriter: One of my playful pastimes when I feel like I am ready to release some resistance in my life is to open up my imagination and pretend I am a cartoon screenwriter. I used to enjoy watching *The Simpsons*. I liked how they took everyday life and exaggerated it until it was ridiculous and humorous.

You, too, can become a cartoon writer and script out your life in such a way you can see the craziness within it — in the process, you release your worries and no longer own them. Make it up like a cartoon you invented, or use your favorite cartoon. Are you Bugs Bunny or Daffy Duck? I feel like I am as wild, crazy, and at times, misunderstood as Daffy is. When I get really excited — which is at least once a day! — I feel like jumping around like Daffy.

Video Game Time: All my boys love to play video games. Even several of my adult friends enjoy mastering a video game when possible. When Mitchel and Carter get a new video game, they will play it for hours. Did I say hours? I meant hours and *days* if necessary.

As an adult, unless you are a video game creator or tester, you may not have several hours straight to play like you want to. If gaming is play for you, I suggest you schedule vacation time or clear out a weekend when you know a new game you want will be released. Go buy that new game, shut out all distractions and play through as many hours as possible on your gaming vacation.

Movie and Dinner: Okay, so seeing a movie may not sound like much fun to some, but for me and a few of my close friends, movies are part of our imaginative play. A couple I know goes out to the movies every Friday night and then to a wonderful dinner. This is something they find fun and enjoyable to do together.

I personally love to see movies all by myself. Talking is also something I love to do and if I go to a movie with others I always want to talk, so I go alone. This is also my opportunity to enjoy and get to know myself more.

Since I enjoy eating a diet consisting of fresh fruits and vegetables and, unfortunately, movie theaters do not provide these fresh options, I smuggle in my own food. I will either head over to the local fresh foods market and pick up some salsa and lettuce, fresh fruit, like a bag of grapes (one of the best popcorn replacements) or if I am feeling particularly hungry, I may order out a raw "burger" or cabbage-filled "taco" from our local raw food restaurant. People around me are always inspired by my fresh, whole foods fare. Take along, or smuggle in, your favorite restaurant food instead of popcorn, pop and candy.

Pajama Day: Hooray for Pajama Day! When you were a kid, didn't you just love to hang out in your pajamas all day? When I was in school, we used to have a read-a-thon every month or so. We could come to school in our pajamas, bring snacks and hang out reading all day. Now to be honest, I did not enjoy reading then like I do today — what I really enjoyed about the read-a-thon was the pajamas, snacks and free time.

If a lazy day sounds fun to you, perhaps you may be inspired to take a day off, hang out in your pajamas all day and rent movies or read a new book. Pretend it is a day off school (work). You can eat what you want, go to the store in your pajamas or robe (if you can), and do whatever else you feel inspired to do in your pajamas. A fun friend of mine even went to a small conference in her pajamas, just because she feels so free being in her PJs.

Go Play Stop ~ Entertain Me

Dance: I sent out a text, tweet and Face Book update asking my friends to inspire me with how they like to play. The number one response among women was dancing. Perhaps I naturally attracted this response because dancing is one of my all-time-favorite playful activities. I am not sure if I am a great dancer or not, but I don't care — I love to dance and feel so playful and free when I do.

I have an abundance of friends who love dancing as much as or more than I do. Whether you dance for fun, or even if you love to compete, it doesn't matter. As long as there has been a drum to beat or a mouth to sing, dancing has been a central part of who we are. Animals of all kind dance, play and flow with the rhythm of life.

Whether you think you are a great dancer or say you don't have rhythm, let go of those beliefs and release your playful spirit through dance. Start playing some fun music loudly enough to feel it in your heart and soul, right in the comfort of your own home, and let loose. Eventually, the rhythm and beat of the music will take you over and your playful spirit will start dancing and leading you along.

Play with Music: Are you the kind of person who loves to play musical instruments, compose lyrics or write music? Perhaps you love to sing and even change the words of your favorite song. Music is so fun to play around with; if you're like me, the pure enjoyment of listening to music is all you need to raise your vibration and get you in the playful mood. (There is more about your vibration in the next chapter.)

There are many ways to play with music — change the words to a song, sing it your way or stand in front of the mirror and sing like a superstar. Many people are gaining an audience on YouTube by posting videos of them singing another artist's music. If you feel like playfully entertaining, take your music or musical instrument to the park with you and play and/or sing for those at the park. You get a playful time to perform and they get to enjoy your musical talents.

Several people throughout the years have shared with me that listening to their favorite music transports them to a new space. Great music can raise your vibration (your mood) and can help you to be a part of the moment you are in now! Take music along wherever you go and create a new space to have fun and even move your body to the beat of the rhythm. Music can be a win-win for facilitating a strong connection with others and allowing each of you to let go of stress easily.

Concert: Live concerts are so fun to attend because the energy of the audience adds to the experience. If you haven't been to a concert in a long time, then now is the best time to go. You could go see a band you once liked years ago if they're still touring. Pretending to be a teenager again is a great game to entertain you — dress up like a rocking or rapping cool teenager again. Let go and be youthful! Play the part, get out of your boring comfort zone and get wild and crazy.

Make Your Own Reality Show: My boys really like to watch various Food Network bake- or cooks-offs. When I started filming my YouTube videos back in 2009, I loved getting up in front of the camera and talking about food and how to make various raw food recipes. Why not get really playfully creative and film a reality show of your own? You could invite a few friends over who also love to cook, bake or create recipes. Invite other friends to be judges and someone to film your reality food party.

If you love animals, create a nature or animal-lovers show by filming your furry or feathered friends. Let your inspiration be your guide and enjoy your playful reality show experience.

See a Play: Plays can be so entertaining, whether you're into dramatic comedies, tragedies or romance. A live play offers you a change from the usual movie and popcorn night. No matter what your budget or where you reside, from New York to L.A., Paris to Rome, from a local high school play to Broadway, you can be magically transformed in a playful experience.

Act in a Play: I love to go beyond being a spectator and be a part of the experience. If you feel the pull to get up on stage and perform in a play, find a local theater and act away. How exciting to be a part of entertaining others in a live presentation! Acting gives you a chance to practice or develop your talent, entertain others, and you get to play with others who love to play. Now that's surrounding you with some fun players in the world.

Talent Show: When I was 14 years of age, I participated in our junior high school talent show. Back in those days, the Super Bowl Shuffle was all the rage. I had an idea to get a bunch of my friends and create our own Super Bowl Shuffle, girl style. We all dressed up in football jerseys, sweats and created our own dance. We won the talent show, and most of all, we had the best time dancing on stage as the "Super Bowl Shuffling Girls."

Find a talent show to be a part of. We all have a talent and no matter what yours is, stretch yourself and show others just how amazingly talented you are. If you can't find a local talent show, you could host your own. Get a group of your friends together and have a Talent Show Party.

Become Your favorite Character: While out on my run one day, I was greeted by a man on a bike. He asked me if I was training for something. I told him I originally wanted to run the Las Vegas Rock n' Roll Marathon but felt so inspired to run, now I only want to run for enjoyment. He shared with me that he would be running in that marathon, dressed up in full costume as Elvis. He loved Elvis and honors him every year by dressing up as him and running the complete Las Vegas marathon. I thought to myself, *what a true player,* and his idea got my imagination flowing.

What a great idea, to dress up like your favorite person or character for a day and run a race or simply go shopping or play around town entertaining people from your creative, playful persona. You get to have fun and play around with a different identity. Who needs Halloween to dress up and play around? Any day is the perfect day to play!

Attend or Create a Comedy Show: Las Vegas has a local comedy improv group that is both fun and includes sponta- neous acting. We attend the show every month and because it is famous for "clean burning comedy" — our children get to come along as well. Comedy is a standard form of play in our home. My husband, Blake, is one of the funniest people I know; his true talent and passion in life is making people laugh.

Not long ago, Blake was turning 50 years old, and for years he had dreamed of being a professional comedian on stage. I really love to support him and wanted to make his dream come true. I asked him if he would be willing to pre- sent his comedy to a group of our friends. He agreed and Blake's comedy-show-and-birthday party was in play.

We invited all of our friends, my husband's co-workers, and because it was another friend's birthday too, we in- cluded him and his friends. We set up a microphone, speak- ers and a stage. Blake prepared his material for weeks, or rather for the past 50 years, and he entertained us all. That night had to be one of the funniest times in my life. I never laughed so much, as did everyone there — about 40 people altogether. Have a playfully funny experience and attend a comedy show or, even better, create your own.

Go Play Stop ~ Big Time Players

A New Language and a Trip: Plan a trip to somewhere you have never been, where you don't know the language, and then learn the language. Practice speaking this new language for 20-60 minutes every day until you leave to go on your trip.

For more assistance in learning the new language, check out Meetup.com and see if there is a local community that meets and speaks the language you are learning and join them. You can let them know you are learning this new language so you can go visit their country. Most people take pride in the country they came from and generally they will be more than happy, excited even, to help you learn.

Who knows, your new friends may even suggest the best places to visit on your trip, along with fun things to do while you are there. Even if you are on a budget and realistically think that you can't afford to go, simply imagine you already have the money, plan the trip and learn the language anyway. If you feel excited and start to believe you are really going, the money or opportunity will always show up to support you.

Rent Fun: For your birthday or any special occasion, tell your loved ones that instead of presents, all you want is money to rent a boat, jet ski, exotic car or motorcycle. Your friends and family love to get ideas for special occasions and will be happy to support you. When you rent your dream-mobile, enjoy the experience as if you just bought it. While driving it or riding in it, feel the excitement, confidence and exhilaration of owning this fun-mobile and completely immerse yourself in the experience.

Take pictures for memories and to remind you how wonderful it felt to be in that moment. Focus on the feeling and thought of owning this machine as much as possible and witness how the Universe will play to make your dream come true.

"Come as You Already Are" Party: Years ago, I read about someone who attended a "Come as You Already Are"

Party in which the participants were invited to pretend they were already what, who or had what they wanted. If you wanted to be a successful real estate owner, you would come to the party dressed the part and speaking the part as if you were already all that. You would have conversations with people about the properties you owned and talk about how well your life is going because of your investments.

I thought this idea sounded like so much fun, I invited seven of my friends over for a "come as if all your dreams have come true" party. For the party, I dressed up as a play fairy, complete with a flowing sparkly dress and wings. Then I gave out business cards with "Playful Fairy" printed on them along with a description of my services. I asked everyone to forward me a description of their dream life so I could keep them on track as well.

We had a great time and within just a few months, each one of my friends had parts of their dream life start to align with their reality. When you feel and act the part of what you want to create, the Universe "shows up" to bring it into your reality.

Beach for a Day: Do you enjoy the sounds and ambiance of waves crashing up on shore or the sounds of seagulls up above? Perhaps you would love to ride a wave, surfing or boogie boarding. Years ago, I worked for an airline and could fly anywhere I wanted on stand-by. One day, I had an inspiring idea to take my kids and fly to the beach for the day.

We flew to San Diego and took a bus to the beach. The kids and I had a blast playing on the beach and when the sun went down, we caught the bus back to the airport and came back home. I thought of how great it would be if this was something we could do anytime, to anywhere.

One of our savings accounts is set up just for spontaneous fun. With the relatively low price of airline tickets, we can easily take a flight to our favorite fun spot and rent a car for the day or take a shuttle to our destination. Create more spontaneous play by hitting the beach for the day or hiking in the Rocky Mountains in Colorado — whatever you do, you will have playful memories to last a lifetime.

Move to Another Country: Have you thought of visiting another country for an extended stay? I recently read about a couple of school teachers who saved money and planned to spend their summer vacation living in South America. My friend Rebecca saved $100 a week for five years and was able to spend eight weeks in France with her husband.

By living somewhere instead of just visiting, you will get to know another culture and country much more because you'll have time to relax and slowly enjoy the journey. In addition, if this is a country in which they speak another language, this is the perfect time to learn the language, when it is constantly in your ear. There are so many fun, playful possibilities when you become a part of the culture rather than a tourist for a few days or a week. Get to know yourself more and explore a new country by briefly living there.

Long Road Trip: Have you dreamed about touring the United States, Canada, Europe or anywhere you have a thirst to go? How about a road trip? I have a number of friends who travel around the US in an RV. They own and run websites, travel around entertaining or selling various items at shows, and which allows them the freedom to travel.

They enjoy traveling with the weather — visiting the northern states in the summer months and southern states in the winter time. One family took their twin boys and biked across the United States and two years later, they biked from Canada to Argentina. They have had so many playful adventures and met many different, amazing people along the way.

Freedom is a way of life for these families, couples and individuals. The road is their home and they live in the moment enjoying the journey. If your dream is to see and experience more of the world, you too can free yourself up for more playful traveling in the world.

A Fun, New Career: One of my deepest passions is to see people loving themselves so much, they play through their lives, doing what they love and loving what they do in every area, and especially in their career. Maybe this is such a passion of mine because I personally know what it is like to work at a job that did not match who I am as a person.

What if you don't know what you want to do and do not feel inspired at this time in your life? It's time to try a new, playful career on for size. I have dedicated a whole chapter to the subject of inspired careers (Chapter 7) because we tend to spend more time working to financially support ourselves than anything else. My vision is that we can blur the lines between work and play until our work becomes our play and our play becomes our work.

What better way to live than from inspiration? If you are living from passion and inspiration, success and money will follow. When you are living in your *why* — your inspired reason for living — others automatically want to jump in and support you. Perhaps for now, start creating a vision of a new, fun career. Try on jobs that look inspiring. For example, if you love to hike, work for a hiking tour company for a time and you will know quickly if it is for you or not.

If you know what you want to do, but are limited in the number of hours in a day you have to pursue it, there is always a way to start entering your chosen field, even if it is only one day or a few hours a week. The more excited you become about your new career path, the more the Universe will open doors to make it happen for you.

Learn to Fly: "The sky's the limit!" If you're in for a high-flying, playful time, why not learn to fly? It is fairly easy to get your private pilot's license and fly for fun or to go places in sky-style. Three friends of ours all decided to get their pilots license and then purchased a small aircraft together. They created a timeshare agreement for their aircraft and take turns playing in the sky. Find out more about the nearest local flying club; some of them have very good deals for renting airplanes once you have your license.

If you have wanted to play like a bird and fly, now is always the best time to set your sights high and make your plans to take flight.

Long Boat Trip: Have you ever played around with the idea of sailing on the ocean or boating to Hawaii? The ocean is open, free and full of playful characters like dolphins and whales. Imagine the adventure and excitement of the water, the wind, and you out there on the water — perhaps with others, or maybe just you and your thoughts.

There are many wonderful, entertaining stories and blogs of people who are out there, living their lives out on the ocean fulfilling their dreams. They sail from island to island, port to port, visiting new spaces and seeing new faces. Their course is set and their passion is in full swing as they enjoy each moment out in the open air. If this sounds inspiring to you, find out more; there is plenty of information and inspiration that so many are willing to share.

* * *

I hope these different examples — "sparks of inspiration" — excite you with a few ways you can begin to play more. The only limits are in your imagination. Stretch your mind and your creative power. I promise, once you have opened yourself up to play, an abundance of playful ideas and opportunities will come your way. The moment I started wanting to inspire others to play more, playful people showed up in my life asking me to play. Every day, in every way, there is always a moment to allow your spirit to come out and play!

4

PLAYING WITH MONEY

Why Play!
As you play you will thrive,
not just survive.

Abundance in All Things

Isn't it fun to toy around with the idea of abundance, wealth, prosperity and money? Have you ever seen a car or house you would just love to buy? Perhaps you'd like to go on a vacation, retire early or simply feel the freedom of purchasing anything you would like without ever having to look at the price tag.

What would happen in your life if for a day, a week, a month or even a year, you started playing with your thoughts and saw the world around you as *abundant,* and you trusted in the higher power of the Universe to take care of all the details of the "how" and all you ever had to do is dream, feel good and play?

We all have had dreams of more money, more things and more opportunities to create more abundance in our life. Why is it that the wealth in the world resides in the hands of less than 1% of the population? Money is so central to our experience and yet most of us feel as if we never have enough.

I am sure you have your own personal reasons for why you feel you do not have enough money, as most of us do. You could blame it on anything from your genes, to the government, or those that are already wealthy. But what really is money? Money is no more than energy and paper or coins with some kind of value attached to them, used in exchange for goods or services. Money should be no harder to attract than a peanut butter and jelly sandwich. Imagine if we thought of it in those terms. Who knows what possibilities lay ahead of us if only we could learn the game of money and play it to win?

This playful abundant chapter is one I couldn't wait to share with you. My own personal relationship with money has changed greatly because of my mental, emotional and spiritual shift, combined with playing a whole new money game. I used to think "Who needs money? I bet I could learn to live without it. Sure, I would really like to be wealthy but I don't know how." I had a thousand more excuses, and even though I have spent thirty years wanting to be rich and re-searching the wealthy, I had contradictory beliefs that kept me living paycheck to paycheck.

This thought keeps coming up from my intuition: *What if you really understood just how powerful you are... what would you create?*

While in the shower one day, I had an inspired idea, a vision. All I could see was gentle, loving hands holding out a silver platter. On the platter was all the money, cars, houses — everything — all the stuff I had ever asked for. A voice said "the Universe is holding out its hands to you, to give you all you have ever asked for and all you need to do is *be* and feel happy about your life, with or without the stuff. The rela-tionships, money and stuff you want are already around you; when you feel good, you will begin to recognize it, see it clearly and attract more."

Then I received this thought: "It does not matter if you ask for $10, $100, $1000 or a *billion* dollars, the Source within you and the Universe, say *Yes!*" I thought about this for a moment and how it related to play. We all play with money and the games we play either support us or we may think we are losing the money game altogether.

I, for one, will admit that I have pushed money away and allowed just enough into my reality to get by. There have been times in my life when I felt I had lost the money game and had to hit the restart button (bankruptcy), and wouldn't you know it, I just came back and played the same game again, in the same way.

What is amazing, though, is that **abundance is always there**, no matter how we play the money game. Similar to the game of Monopoly, we have the opportunity to come back and play it again as many times as we like. How many of us have read stories of famous people like Donald Trump who came back after losing all his wealth or Christopher Gardner (Pursuit of Happyness), who was once homeless, living on the street with his young son, to become wealthy. All they did was allow abundance, or rather get out of the way, and play the money game to win. I've spent some time shifting my own vibration, energy and relationship to the abundance in all things, including money and you can do it too.

Your Vibrational Signal

Your vibration is how you communicate with the Universe and others. Simply put, vibration is a vibe or signal you put out through your thoughts and emotions which brings forth or *attracts* things into your life — what you want and, at times, what you don't want. This is the basis of the Law of Attraction.

Here are a couple of examples: when you feel confident and joyful, the Universe gives you a joyful experience with a friend or perhaps a refund check comes in the mail unexpectedly. If you are feeling sad or angry about a subject, the next thing you know, you trip and fall or your car breaks down.

What you think and feel sends out a vibrational wave or signal and what you receive in return matches that vibrational signal. This is why it is important to think thoughts that cause you to feel playful, joyous and free as much as possible because doing so will bring you more experiences that are playful, joyous and free.

My friend Joan describes the Law of Attraction so simply. Imagine a toy paddleball, like the kind you may have had when you were younger. The rubber ball is attached to an elastic band and the other end of the elastic band is attached to the paddle. The paddle represents you, the ball represents your thoughts-with-feelings, or vibrations, and the elastic band is the Universe. As you hit the ball, the elastic band brings it right back to the paddle. A fleeting thought won't set up a very strong vibration — if you hit the ball weakly it won't generally hit the paddle — but thoughts and feelings that you think/feel often, or "practice," especially when they bring up strong emotions, will set the tone of your vibration — like hitting the ball hard — and, therefore, experiences come into your life to match that vibration. Often times, the result comes quickly with full force.

Connecting to Abundance

I live in small town surrounded by nature. Mountains, wild animals and desert plants are always in abundance. One afternoon while I was out on a hike, I started to be aware of just how abundant nature is. Everywhere I walked, I saw wildlife, like rabbits or snakes of some sort. There were plants of the same species in more abundance than I could count. While noticing all this abundance, I began to sense the feeling of abundance and appreciation wash over me — I was finally seeing abundance in a whole new way and the amazing part is, it was always there, regardless of my awareness of it.

Go Play Stop ~ The Pay, Save and Appreciate Game

Paying your bills and saving money doesn't necessarily sound like a game, at least not to a spender like me. Isn't it interesting how when you change your perspective, saving money and paying credit cards can become playful and fun with the right attitude? Watching just one credit card go down and your savings go up at the same time can be both rewarding and exciting.

After facing the possibility of bankruptcy for the third time in my twenty years of adult life, I made a firm decision that it was time for me to learn the money game and get abundant! Over the course of several days, I was guided with clues on how to play this money game more productively, to shift my vibration and to change my relationship with money as well as the abundance in all things.

Step #1: Pay: I felt strongly inspired to keeping paying my bills, focusing on paying off one credit card at a time, starting with the card with the lowest balance. At that point, we had accumulated in excess of $6,000 dollars in credit card debt with four separate credit cards. It felt good to start with the lowest balance of $500 because I could see results quickly.

Step #2: Save. I noticed a book on my shelf that I had never read by T. Harv Eker called *The Millionaire Mind*, so I read it. He suggests that you start saving money in several separate money jars or bank accounts. He says "start with even a dollar in each account and work your way up to 10% or more of your income." I felt my intuition agree with this saving system, so I set up six separate savings accounts that I could easily transfer money into weekly and named each account:

1. Financial Freedom
2. New Vehicle
3. Play
4. Education
5. Contingency
6. Pay Credit Cards Off

Even Eker suggests a "Play" account because he understands the importance of play too.

To be honest, at that point, I had never been a saver and had only ever paid the minimum payments on my credit cards. Over the past 25 years of earning money, I had only saved for a short time and was always in debt or getting back into debt. So, there I was, at 40, being inspired with a new way to play the money game.

My intuition continued to let me know that it wasn't the actual action of paying off the credit cards or saving money that was the most important part; it was the shift in my focus. The most important aspect was how I would feel while watching the credit cards decrease and the savings increase. These feelings of accomplishment and ease would align my vibration and allow more abundance to come forth easily without much effort from me.

Step #3: Appreciate: The third and most important part of the money game is simple, and yet it takes more emotional and mental awareness than the other two action steps. Appreciation of the abundance in what you already have will create the largest shift in your vibration. Appreciation is the feeling of abundance. It will support you in moving from where you are now to where you want to be financially, and it will bring abundance — in all things — into your experience easily while at the same time relieving and releasing the stress around money.

Because I was not the primary financial supporter in our family, I began to appreciate all the wealth and abundance my husband worked so hard to create. As each paycheck was deposited into our bank account, I would show appreciation to him personally and to the Universe for all it provided in our life. I would enjoy the thoughts of how it easily just showed up every week like magic in our bank account, and how this money allowed us the ability and *freedom* to pay our bills, save money, pay for our living expenses and more.

I started to feel abundant, wealthy and rich. The more I felt this way and focused on it, the more easily it appeared that I had more than enough money to pay all our living expenses, credit cards, save money and have extra left over.

Winning the Pay, Save and Appreciate Game: One year after starting this playful money game, the credit cards were paid in full and with the money I saved, we paid cash for a second vehicle, went on two family vacations, and we were able to easily pay for emergency car maintenance. More importantly, money from my business and unexpected sources began to trickle in and kept flowing in more each month.

Like rain drops before the storm, I feel the storm of abundance in all things beginning to pour down into my life without much effort. I did nothing more than:

1. Made a conscious decision to change to a playful attitude.
2. Played with my credit card balances.
3. Enjoyed the excitement of watching my savings grow.
4. Focused on the feeling of abundance with the current flow of money coming.
5. Then, as more money came forth, I would feel overjoyed with eager anticipation of *even more* that was coming easily, trusting that the Universe would continue to provide more without any extra action from me.

Go Play Stop ~ Game Playing

Cash Flow For Kids, by famous author Robert Kiyosaki, is a children's game our boys love to play with us. In the game, each player is represented by a colorful rat who tries to get out of the infamous Rat Race. The object of the game is to get more passive income than debts. The game is fun and it gives you a fairly accurate picture of where your money mind is at. Mitchel and Carter almost always win because children think in abundance, while my husband and I usually come in last.

The game is played by rolling the dice. What I find interesting is that the roll of the dice is strictly chance, right? Or is it? If each player has the opportunity to win, why is it that the people playing the game who are in debt, in this case my husband and I, tend to roll just the right amount on the dice to land on the debt spaces, whereas the kids, who have no limiting beliefs around money, rarely, if ever, seem to land on the debt spaces and always land on pay day or investment opportunities. It isn't chance at all — it's vibration.

There are also two adult versions of this game, but for simplicity, I enjoy playing the children's version of the game, simply to see where my financial mindset is. We have had this game for years, and once I started saving, paying off my debts and enjoying a new mindset of abundance, I landed less and less on the debt spaces. One time, I even came in second.

There are many financial board games out on the market today like Cash Flow, Monopoly and an MLM game called Residual Income. Playing them is a great way you can test your financial mindset and have fun unconsciously learning new wealth-building skills. Because your brain doesn't care if it is real or not, playing these games can unconsciously change your thinking about money. In addition, your feeling of wealth and ease of creating abundance within a playful setting will also allow the Universe to bring money directly to you.

Go Play Stop ~ Believe, Ask and Release

After my husband and I agreed we would eventually separate from our relationship and that I would be supporting myself and creating my own life wealth, I felt a sudden rush of fear and doubt come over me. One day as I was heading back from my walk, I asked myself and my inner guidance, "will I really be able to financially support myself?" Within seconds I received an answer. I looked down to find a dime in my path, and I heard a voice say, "Yes, and more than you know right now."

Believe It or Not: I have personally experienced the power of the Universe to provide everything I need and want, and answers to all my questions. We all have the opportunity to play with the Universe by believing in It and ourselves. The Universe, God or Source, will automatically match you with experiences that align with your vibrational output *whether you believe in it or not.*

One of the playful things I love to do is see the Universe as my own personal assistant. Doing this helps me to be aware of my thoughts and emotions. My number one intention each and every day is to pay attention to the way I feel. I want to feel good, happy and joyful every day in every way possible. As long as I am feeling good, I have no *work* to do, but the moment I begin to experience negative emotions, my work, or rather *play*, is to find a new perspective to view the situation from, so that I can feel good.

By practicing on focusing as much as I can on what any negative emotion has caused me to desire, and then turning my attention towards the outcome of that desire, my vibration shifts. I feel the shift and see how everything in my life begins to change right before my eyes. When I do this process with a playful attitude or treat the emotion like part of a game, I end up playing through my life and my vibration is very playful.

Simply imagine you are the creator of your financial reality as if it was a video game and the object of the game is to shift your vibration and become a match to your wealth. Wealth is chasing you and if you, the player, can either align by collecting the feeling of wealth or abundance, or shift your negative vibration to a positive one, then you align with the wealth and win the game, becoming financially abundant.

Ask and Play Attention: There are days when I can't seem to understand some experience, person or situation in my life so I ask the Universe. Like the example of my dime story above, you too can ask your "Universal Assistant" to bring abundance into your reality, or anything else for that matter. (There is more about Universal Assistants in Chapter 7.) Asking the Universe with your feelings and therefore vibration is amazing and perfect because It always answers.

It's easy to pay or *play* attention to what the answer is if you stay aware. We all have a guidance system and this system communicates with us by how we feel. When you think a thought that is in alignment with your inner guidance system, you feel good emotions and your life is in the flow. If however, you are thinking thoughts that are not in alignment with your inner being or guidance system, you feel negative emotions. This is because your inner being does not agree with your negative thought and will not join you in that negative space. Your negative emotion is an indicator that you are not in agreement with who you really are.

Your Intuition or Universal Assistance Communication: Your Universal Assistant will often communicate inspirations to you after you have asked It for assistance. It answers you by providing you with a flash of inspiration in the form of a feeling in your body when you are contemplating a decision. Other times the Universe, your guidance system, or inner being may communicate with you through a voice similar to your own, or you may receive a vision like a movie you haven't seen before, or perhaps just a feeling of *knowing* that you can't explain.

Not everyone will receive all four of these messages — a feeling, a voice, a vision or a knowing — but we all have the ability to feel our emotions. Listen to your feelings — they are part of your inner guidance. You can pay attention when asking for wealth by relaxing and then recording any synchronicities that are going on in your life. When I asked my Universal Assistant if I would be able to financially support myself, I paid attention to the answer. It may have been only a dime, but I know what it meant and heard a *yes.*

At times, you may have had experiences that you view as "bad." Perhaps you lost your job or got in an accident. Keep in mind these are **not** bad experiences — they are actually a part of the abundance coming your way. For example, when my husband informed me that he no longer wanted to be married to me, for months I reacted in sadness and despair. Now I understand that our separation is perfect! I asked for a relationship that was more in alignment with my new values and now the Universe can bring forth a loving partner that will be a better match to me.

To practice playing with your Universal Assistant, start with simple questions you may not know the answer to. For fun one afternoon, my friend, Karen, and I were spending time together and she asked her Universal Assistant, "I would like to see a man wearing a kilt." This question did not have any negative emotional charge around it. In fact, she and I sat around laughing about this expected experience. Within less than a week, while visiting Cincinnati, Ohio, a man walked by her wearing a kilt. Her Universal Assistant answered had answered her giving her what she had asked for.

Release the Resistance, the Stress and Allow: Unlike the kilt example above, money tends to have a negative emotional charge and attachment to it for most people. Usually, it is because we think we have to do some type of action to produce wealth. Another resistance we may have is our lack of belief in ourselves and our worthiness to bring it into existence. We can shift this belief by reaching in and pulling out our playful, child-like spirit and change our beliefs about money.

There is abundance beyond wealth and beyond your human experience. What you think and feel you have or don't have is all the result of your **beliefs**. To explore your beliefs, you can simply ask yourself a few questions, such as "What do I want and why *don't* I have it yet?" The *why* is usually made up of excuses and limiting beliefs we may be unconsciously unaware that we have. We have picked up most of our beliefs from childhood. This is all part of resisting our natural well-being and preventing the abundance in all things to flow into our lives.

The essence in the abundance in one area of your life can bring about the essence of abundance in all things or areas of your life. For example if you have an amazing loving partnership that you love and appreciate and you continually to focus on how much you love and appreciate it, you may find yourself presented with a new career opportunity you will love and appreciate as well. However, unsupportive thoughts and feelings (beliefs) are the lock, or ball-and-chain, you place on yourself that limits your possibilities. When you think a negative thought long enough, it becomes a negative *belief*, and this belief cages you and paves your path and future experiences preventing what you want from coming into your life, and instead brings you more of what you don't want.

Releasing and replacing your unsupportive beliefs with supportive ones can easily occur through play and games. Play allows you to unlock the cage, or ball-and-chain, of limits and sets you free. When you play and have fun you feel good. Creating ways to play through your life affects your attitude, your well-being, and even your health. Ultimately, when you play you naturally become joyful and abundant.

To gain a bit more clarity in your life about the people, stuff, and experiences you wish to have or easily attract, you can jump start your imagination by asking yourself *why* you want what you want. Your deep heart-felt *WHY* is the magic, passion, purpose and heart and soul of what you want and desire. Often times you think that in the getting of these experiences they will ultimately "make" you happy. However, nothing or no one can make you happy and the true key to unlock your full potential is to practice feeling happy without the thing or person you think will "make" you happy. When you can practice feeling joyful without the current desire, your desires will easily show up in your experience automatically.

Start today, in this moment, to practice thinking and feeling about the life you want or all the wonderful aspects of your life you already have manifested. Feel the appreciation, joy and abundance in everything and anything, including experiences, situations and opportunities that you once thought were "bad" that now you realize were always for the best. Your true freedom comes when you can create a way to see life in a playful, fun or even optimist fashion, **no matter what** you are experiencing in the world around you including debt, divorce, or illness.

This may sound crazy, unachievable or nonrealistic; however, I promise you it IS possible to experience and even create the life you want from a deeper, more connected, consciously and purposeful way simply by focusing on ways to play. Keep focused on the things or people in your life or those you wish to come that you love and appreciate and/or any thought that feels good. I personally like to focus on fun childhood experiences if I can't find a better feeling thought in my now reality.

A great way you can think of one positive thought of appreciation and/or love is as one tiny tomato seed. Once the seed is planted in nutrient rich soil (your feeling), given lots of water consistently everyday (you continued drenching of the feel good thought or memory) and along with sunshine (shining your love and appreciate on others) that one little seed gives birth to many tomatoes (more and new experiences, stuff and people who cause you to feel good) and more seeds within those tomatoes for future tomatoes (more wonderful experiences, stuff and people on their way).

Playing can become a very important aspect of your life because even the idea of playing and having fun is the seed that will sprout an abundance of fun, playful and joyful life experiences and people in all areas of your life. This book and the playful processes within it are simply the seeds of inspiration to start your playfully fun garden and, of course, to inspire you to feel good, joyful and abundant. This practice will begin to shift your vibration and head you in a fun direction in your life and in no time you will start to see evidence of this shift through the experiences and people that begin to show up. When you can maintain the essence of well-being consistently and long enough, your life will continue to shift and everything you desire will begin to come faster and more abundant than you can even anticipate.

Go Play Stop ~ Imagining More Playful Abundance Games

If I had only one sign I could carry around with me to remind you (and me) to focus on well-being it would say *Stop Doing and Start Playing!* Through the essence of feeling playful, you will release resistance, feel good and attract all the abundance you desire. This sounds so much "easier said than done" when bills need to be paid, children need attending to, or we are pressured by any of the other demands we've created in our lives. Yet with a playful attitude and perspective, we can include play in every situation, no matter how big or small it feels to us.

In the space of enjoying each moment — being present and playful — are all the answers you seek. Play with money, the idea of money, and believe in your ability to attract it and be wealthy.

Can you really imagine physical dollars to feel abundance? Perhaps a more playful way to feel abundant is to imagine shopping for a new outfit or buying something fun, like a new sports car or a vacation to Hawaii. How do you feel driving that fast new machine or basking in the sun on the beaches of Maui?

Recently, I started playing around with the number 8. The number 8 is the number for abundance or money in numerology and it is the infinity sign as well. A fun game I like to play is to attract the number 8 as a representation of wealth. One 8 means that abundance is getting closer, two 8's are even better but three 8's are the best.

I like to watch out for the number 8 on license plates, billboards, receipts or prices of items while shopping. It is a fun game to play with kids, your mate or any other who wishes to play along. By playing this "8 is Great" game, I have added another way in which to release resistance to money and allow it to flow forth.

Be aware of the abundance you already have and offer it to others. Think about and feel the abundant amount of love you give to those around you. Another sign of abundance is in your mother's smile when she hears your loving words, the gift of a hug to all those you greet, or the energy exchanged in enchanting eye contact. Witness the expansion and abundance in the animals in nature, life in the ocean or trees in the forest.

Think the thoughts and feel the feelings of what wealth and abundance means to you as if you were already living it.

Abundance feels infinite, expansive, invigorating and free. Whatever thoughts allow you to feel excited, loved, boundless, joyful, and in a state of appreciation will give you the feeling of abundance as well.

If you find yourself in a financial situation less than what where you would really enjoy being, then I invite you to join me, together we can shift our beliefs about our worthiness along with our money mindset. The simplest way to create abundance, relationships, health or happiness, is not by your actions but by your beliefs, thoughts and feelings. Freedom and abundance are within your power — simply feel joyful and play, and the doors to your wealth will open wide and all will flow easily to you.

5

THE ART OF FLIRTING

Why Play!
Feeling and being playful
attract playful experiences,
people and possibilities!

Flirting?

Flirting is no more than playing with the connection you have with yourself and another. When two people flirt, or rather, have a wonderful and beautiful connection, they are both in that moment tuned in and turned on to themselves. The more they each continue to connect to themselves, the more they connect to one another. Flirting is not limited to just attraction or rapport with a potential intimate partner — friends flirt and business partners flirt because life is fun and flirty when you're connected.

The connection I am referring to is the connection to your innermost being or higher self — or it may simply be feeling wonderful as you think of another, and appreciating something you enjoy about them. As long as you can maintain the feeling of alignment and connection to yourself, upon approaching another, the interaction flows with ease.

Oftentimes, that is why it is so easy to be in a loving relationship with a person who was previously a friend or co-worker. When we enter into such a relationship, it feels easy because we are not over-thinking ourselves and we aren't nervous or scared about approaching or talking with this friend-plus-more. It is only when we lose our confidence — our connection to our self — that we start to mess up our vibration and either say something we hadn't intended to or feel unworthy to speak to them at all.

The more you open up to and practice flirting with others, the more flirting opportunities will come your way. I have found that as I practice playing as a way of living, more playful experiences and people come my way. Like attracts like; think, feel, and focus on what or who you want, and allow the Universe to do the rest.

Flirting Idea

Recently at a workshop I attended, we were asked to announce our most embarrassing traits loudly in front of the whole class. One particular gentleman whom I considered to be a very attractive and interesting young man announced, "I suck at flirting!" I found this to be rather humorous as did the rest of the class. The whole room laughed, and within seconds we moved on to the next person.

As the day progressed, I couldn't get this young man's comment out of my mind. I thought about how easy and second-nature flirting is for me, and my mind began to race about the idea of flirting. How do people flirt, why do they flirt, and could I teach others to flirt?

We all have a need to feel connected to others — to feel as if we belong — but we must connect and belong to ourselves first. As I have experienced in my own life, we tend to become attached or even addicted to the affection of others. Many of us lost our sense of self as a young child. Most parents, without conscious thought, believe that their children should please them and should behave according to their expectations. This can lead us to look to others for approval, instead of listening and paying attention to that still, small voice within us — a feeling within our body, or the insight and inspiration coming from within, guiding us towards our higher good. We can end up ignoring our inner voice and seeking outside ourselves for guidance.

I found my relationship with my husband to flow so long as I was his object of attention and admiration. After discovering our connection had shifted and he no longer felt a connection to our marriage and, particularly, to me as his mate, I completely lost my sense of who I am! All my life, I had gravitated to men in an attempt to get their appreciation and admiration in order for me to feel good and feel as if I belonged.

All of a sudden, his attention was on another and I could no longer feel good about myself. I lost 25 pounds, which is quite a bit of weight for someone who is only 5 feet 5 inches tall and weighs 130 pounds. I questioned myself, my beauty, my worthiness, and ultimately, I felt as if the "love drug dealer" had cut me off. For the first time in my life, my behavior became that of an addict.

I begged and pleaded for my husband to love me to remember why he loved me. I stopped sleeping more than 2 to 4 hours a night and started starving myself. I even went so far as to contemplate suicide, threatening to drive myself off the Grand Canyon. Only after several months of searching deeply into all human behavior and needs did I realize just how crazy we can become if we do not first relearn to connect and listen to our guidance system and inner being. Start by falling in love and flirting with the person looking back at you in the mirror.

Flirting is a form of playing — playing with the connection you have to yourself, because your life is a reflection of your beliefs, understanding and knowledge of yourself. When you allow yourself to merge with your inner being by abiding in a space of knowing, love and appreciation, you become complete. You feel emotionally full, powerful, confident, and you experience a natural high beyond what any artificial drug or relationship can give you. Once this connection is achieved, you will easily shower others with appreciation and love, plus you will attract the perfect people who match you in connectedness and consciousness as well.

During my own process of transformation from the hurt and pain of my dissolving marriage, I started meditating. I understood the power of mediation and yet I hadn't really thought of it as "playful," until a friend of mine inspired me with her own playful meditative experiment.

Go Play Stop ~ Flirting with the Universe — Creating from Within

Karen, an avid daily meditator, challenged me to join her for a 30-day trial to create our reality from within. I knew this to be completely true, because my own thoughts, emotions and beliefs about myself and others had created the pain I had been living in for the past six months. "The process is simple," she told me:

Meditate for 10 to 15 minutes, creating the connection to your inner being.

Then write down 10 desires you wish to come true in 30 days, and 10 desires you would like to come into your reality over the next year or so.

Now meditate on each item, as if it is already happening, for 68 seconds each.

Do this process morning and night, or at least once a day.

Throughout the day, record all the synchronicities that occur that you may have brought about while focusing on your desires.

She explained how amazing she felt after doing this and it had only been two days. I couldn't wait to do this! With all the struggle and contrast going on in my life, I had already "shot off rockets of desire" for, and had become extremely clear about, what I really wanted!

I immediately started writing down all desires for the next 30 days. In some areas, I was very specific, including dates, times and people involved, and for other items, I was more general as for the total outcome I wanted. About half of my ten desires were business or management and the rest were personal goals and affirmations. I felt inspired, fully alive and eager for the future! I was overflowing with the feeling that I am a conscious, powerful creator and all my dreams come true.

Next, I wrote about the ten things I wanted to attract in the next year. Many of those desires revolved around friend ships, loving people surrounding me, and having an easy, fun, abundant and playful life.

The next morning, I started to apply the process and sure enough, I felt amazing and naturally high during that time and long after. I had never experienced such joy and exhilaration! After a few more days, I could really start to feel the change in my vibration, mood and life. Synchronicities immediately started to show up within an hour of me completing the process. I felt so good, both with the anticipation of my desires coming true and the pure positive connection I was experiencing to myself.

Finally, I could feel the difference between the appreciation and love of another and the appreciation and love of myself. I felt powerful, strong, confident, and connected! Within days, I was able to release my previous, unhealthy attachment to my husband and our relationship. I felt **free** and more "flirty" than I had in the past. I felt full of belonging — no longer to another, but to myself. The next chance I had to flirt with someone, I felt more calm, confident and playful than any other time in my life.

There is no substitute for your inner connection to yourself. Life will become more playful, fun and flirty when you feel connected to yourself!

Breaking the Ice... Forms of Flirting

Flirting with another can come in many forms, from eye contact, to telling a joke or a funny story, a smile, a wink, a friendly conversation or even a "feel-good" thought about another. Flirting is fun and playful, full of genuine care and appreciation for another. Flirting is inspired and full of curiosity to know more about another and, ultimately, to know more about yourself.

True flirting is fancy-free, and comes from a desire to explore what is drawing you towards another. When you are connected with your inner being, feeling relaxed and at ease, your confidence shines through. There are many ways that flirting can be expressed. Use your imagination! Playful flirting has so many possibilities.

How Flirty Can You Be?

As mentioned earlier, flirting is more about the connection you have with yourself than with another person. Once you have mastered or practiced complete alignment with your inner being, flirting comes as naturally and as free-flowing as the wind.

How can you flirt with someone who you may want to get to know more or you feel attracted to?

Step 1. Align with who you really are first; you will attract or be attracted to those "perfect matches" or soul mates with a pure positive connection to themselves as well.

Step 2. Imagine the most amazing relationship or conversation as if it is already happening. You can simply imagine laughing with the person you are attracted to.

Step 3. Approach the person from this high state of being and start a conversation about something you genuinely notice or appreciate about them.

For example, I really enjoy flirting just to bring a smile or light of appreciation into another's day, as well as mine. One day, I watched as two beautiful men with amazing muscle tone were tossing a football back and forth. They were both in their mid- to late-twenties (much younger than I am) and yet I could not help but stare and appreciate their form. As I was about to leave, I gave one of the gentlemen a big flirty smile and walked up to him. I said, "I enjoyed watching you play ball." He replied, "Oh thanks, but we really aren't that good." I couldn't help myself and with a look of complete attraction I said in response, "Oh, I really wasn't paying attention to how you were playing ball. I am enjoying the view of your bodies." He blushed and thanked me. He looked as if he enjoyed the compliment and I thoroughly enjoyed giving it.

I was in perfect alignment with myself, I kept imagining their beauty and form, and then I approached him from a complete space of appreciation about something I enjoyed about him and the other gentleman. I didn't really have any interest in further contact; I was simply passing on my light of appreciation and love to another person. I made a quick connection that left both of us feeling good.

Relationships begin and connections are made anytime you come from a genuine, loving space. You always have the ability to raise the vibration of another by complete appreciation of him or her, and the connection will come easily. This way of flirting is a win-win for both parties — you feel good offering the appreciation and the other person feels good receiving it. The connection is pure and positive.

Connect and Strengthen Your Flirting Muscles

Do you realize that you draw people into your life who mirror you? They are like you, or they reinforce a belief about who you are. Whether you focus on your insecurities or your strengths, you *will* attract people who mirror those aspects. Oftentimes, many of us live in the unconscious space of life, not realizing that our point of attraction is caused by the vibration of our thoughts, emotions and beliefs.

The Law of Attraction states "that which is like unto itself is drawn." In other words, **things that are similar are attracted to each other**. If you want more opportunities to make fun, flirty connections with others who you would really like to attract into your life, then it's time to "get conscious." The best way to "get conscious" is to notice, align with, and appreciate all the qualities you love (or like) about you.

Go Play Stop ~ Flirting with Yourself

Years ago, after constantly asking my husband to take me out on a date and him making excuses about why he couldn't, I decided to take myself out. I got dressed up, put on my sexiest clothes and headed out to have a delightful dinner with *me!* I drove myself to an elegant restaurant and ordered a delicious meal. Next, I started having a conversation with myself (this conversation was in my head as they may have kicked me out or admitted me into the local mental institution had I spoken to myself out loud).

My thoughts started to wander, and I began to wonder: "Who am I? Why do people enjoy being with me? What do I have to offer in a relationship?" I took out a piece of paper and started to answer myself. I looked at myself from a third person perspective and uncovered a new "me." I wrote:

I am fun!

I have a great smile.

I genuinely care for others.

I want others to be free to make their own choices, rather than forcing them to think like I do

I adore those I spend time with and enjoy taking care of them, making food for them and talking with them about their hopes and dreams.

I love a variety of music, culture and diversity.

I am an excellent lover.

I am...

After an hour of sitting in the restaurant, enjoying my food and conversation with myself, I realized just how amazing I was! I felt so good and so in love with me! I had a pure positive perspective of myself and I felt complete confidence!

"Flirting with yourself" is a wonderful process to raise your vibration, connect to yourself, and get clarity about who you are and what you would like to attract. You, too, can take yourself out and start writing down your best qualities as if you are thinking from another's perspective. Why would someone want to be your partner, mate or even friend? Get as clear as you can and understand that your relationships are no more than a reflection of what you think and feel about yourself.

When you attract amazingly fun, friendly, loving relationships that is all the feedback you need to get to know yourself better and you can feel good that you are creating that. When the relationships are not supportive, know that this is only an opportunity to re-align with your thoughts and feel-ings about yourself — connect to pure, positive energy. It seems like an easy process, but what if you are uncomfort-able looking at yourself? Try the next *Go Play Stop.*

Go Play Stop ~ Flirting with Your Mirrors

Another easy process of connecting with yourself I call "Flirting with Your Mirrors." Again, find a time and space you can be alone to think and "get conscious!" Start to think about the various close relationships you cur-rently have in your life and what you love, like or appreciate in each one. On a piece of paper or in a journal, write down the first person's name and then list all the qualities you en-joy about them. Then go on to the second, third and so forth until you can't think of any other person you enjoy being with.

When you feel complete, look over the list a second time and cross out each name and place your name there in-stead. These are all the qualities you have within you, quali-ties you are similar to, and/or things that you believe you de-serve in your life. Over the years, the more I have done this mirror process — looking at my friends or even those I may not currently enjoy — the more I learn about myself and get feedback on how I can become more aware and conscious of my thoughts, emotions, behaviors and beliefs.

Years ago, in my late teens and early 20's, I had a friend who I loved, but I never felt comfortable in our relationship. She constantly put demands on me and took me for granted. She would make up rules about our friendship and tell me if I didn't do such-and-such then she wouldn't be my friend.

One day she accused me of doing something behind her back. I felt so sad as I walked away crying, and then I real-ized I could no longer be friends with someone who believed I would do something like that. Years later, I came to under-stand that I believed I was not worthy enough to have loving relationships. I went many years without close friendships before I started getting clear about who I was and what I deserved.

Today, I am a match for and attract into my life the most amazing, loving, and caring relationships. I know the more I have expanded and allowed my worthiness in, the better my current friendships are and the more amazing new relationships are as well. Now, when I look at the qualities of the people that surround me — my mirrors — I know how much better I think and feel about myself.

Flirting with the Future

Looking into the future, you have the opportunity to be confident, self-assured, and walk up to anyone and make a delicious connection. You have the ability to see your life as fun and flirty, making connections in various forms along your way. You have nothing to worry about — just stay connected and play your way through in the most life has to offer.

Smile more, make eye contact and offer words, or even thoughts, of appreciation of yourself and another. Look in the mirror and flirt with you. Tell a stranger (just a friend you haven't met yet!) how much you appreciate the way he or she looks, their hair, or their smile. Once you are clear about yourself, open up and notice the opportunities you have to consciously connect with others.

For a few months I had started giving close attention to my fitness and health. I was practicing my appreciation of my new figure, form and "flirting" with myself in the mirror. While shopping for clothes one afternoon, I walked in the store the same time as a woman who was shopping with her teenage daughter, for a brief moment we both smiled at one another and made a connection with deep eye contact. Without words, I felt as if we were both sending appreciation and love to one another. Moments later, as I was looking through the beautiful clothes on the rack and feeling so wonderful, she came up to me and told me how great she thought my body looked. She said, "I know how hard it can be to stay in shape and I just wanted you to know that I noticed." I thanked her and felt so amazing simply from her appreciation of what I was mirroring in her (her body was also very beautiful).

Understand that no one person can *make* you happy, but each one of us can show kindness, love, and be an example of what it means to be connected, fun and flirty!

6

CREATING PLAYFUL LOVING RELATIONSHIPS

Why Play!
Playing with others creates
deeper, stronger, more joyful connections!

Partner Play Time

My husband, Rod, and I have been married over 36 years. We discovered early on in our marriage to schedule in "together" fun. We have always made time to have fun together. Sometimes it was challenging to do so because life got in the way. However, we made that time.

Our youngest, Lance, went off to college nearly 12 years ago. Yes, we felt the heartache of having an empty nest. As one chapter in our life ended, a new one began. We soon discovered the benefits of having an empty nest. One of those benefits was it freed us to play more often. We took up hobbies and tried new adventures. Yes, we finally had time and could afford to see the world together.

Our first fun trip together "just us" was to Mexico to our timeshare in Puerto Vallarta. We had a blast! No kids and just us playing and doing what we wanted to do. The fun time in Mexico motivated us to schedule additional trips to places we had only dreamed of going while we were raising our family. On these trips, my thing is taking pictures of the amazing sights and Rod's thing is trying all the local cuisine. We both love the sight-seeing and mingling with the locals.

We have traveled together to Ireland, Costa Rica, Tahiti, Easter Island, Peru, China, Hong Kong, and Japan, to name a few. We are not done playing yet — off to Korea in a few months to visit my older son and his family, and next year we will go to Africa for a photography safari to celebrate our 60th year on this planet!

It is never too late to have fun together. I truly believe having fun together has fueled our love for each other and it is one of the many reasons we have a happy and long marriage.

Vicki Kallman

Please note: This chapter is not just for couples — single people will find inspiration and practical tools to help them, too!

Personal intimate relationships or partnerships offer us the opportunity to get to know another person and ourselves more deeply than is possible in any other type of relationship. In personal relationships, we get close, up front and personal; at times, we even show sides of ourselves we may never show to another. We tell and share secrets. We also share our physical bodies and our emotions. Sometimes, we may even experience such a powerful connection with the one we love, we feel as if we are one complete person instead of two separate beings.

If you haven't experienced the feeling of being "in love" to the point that you reflect the highest form of you — a relationship of complete appreciation and love — then open up and take the plunge. You do have the opportunity; there is someone, or perhaps many "someones," who you can really immerse yourself in and fall deeply in love with. When you do, your life will take on a whole new light. You will feel euphoric, almost high, from the exchange of love, connection and affection between the two of you.

Over the years, I have attracted several different forms of personal relationships into my life. Each one of them felt unique in its own way and until Blake came along when I was 26, I had never really allowed myself to experience the immersion of the "in-love high." The in-love high comes from a complete, pure positive connection to another. You are aligned with your inner being, they are aligned with theirs, and then each of you completely showers the other with appreciation — the reflection becomes one. In this love exchange — the flood of appreciation and pure positive connection — the one you love becomes the object of your attention and you, theirs.

After experiencing this myself, I completely understand why people who fall in love no longer have a sense of time, space or reality. The couple is completely connected, tuned in, turned on and living in the euphoria of what feels like timeless magic. Colors seem brighter, the sky seems bigger and the world is vast — anything seems possible.

You feel passionate and are inspired to create works of art, climb the highest mountain and do what once seemed impossible, because you are living in that space of pure love. Love can cause you to feel limitless and raise your vibration beyond what you may have previously felt. If you have experienced the love connection, then you also know the power of connecting with your inner being and the worthiness of who you really are.

The Flame of Passion

If you are currently having an in-love experience, this is the perfect time to start cultivating a playful, loving relationship with your mate. Passion is alive and you are both in a creative space to get to know each other on the deepest level. For those in a personal relationship that has lost the fire, or if you are not currently in a romantic relationship but are eagerly anticipating one to come, you are in a wonderful place as well. For those of you looking to rekindle the passion you once had with your partner, I'll show you ways to spice it up through play, attention and appreciation! If you are one of many who are looking for and hopefully open to the possibility of a playful, loving and passionate relationship coming into your life, you can have all you want within a thought and feeling!

Go Play Stop ~ Keeping Passionate Love Playfully Alive

For those in the midst of a passionate, loving relationship, you are reading this book at the perfect time; you have the opportunity to keep the flame going for years to come. The process is easier during this period because you are already clear about what you want, and you're living in the manifestation of what you have created and allowed into your experience.

Playful Loving Steps to Keep the Passion Burning

Step 1. Without over-thinking, take a few moments to notice what really inspires you about your partner. What are the qualities you see within him or her and the traits that you appreciate about them? What do they do that lets you know you are loved by this person and how do you show love towards them?

Is it the way they **physically touch** you that inspires you? Do you enjoy all aspects of touch and not just the sex? For example: You like the massages, holding hands, hugs and other ways they touch you, whether you are together in public or in private.

Is it the **acts of service** they do for you? For example, when you say, "I'm cold," they literally give you the shirt or jacket off their back or bring you a blanket to give you warmth.

Do you enjoy the **gifts** they give you or the **gift of presence** they provide? For example, do you like the way they surprise you with gifts that excite you? Or is it the complete attention they bestow upon you, putting all things aside and enjoying just you?

You may feel especially loved when they spend **quality time** with you and give you their undivided attention. Or is it the places you go to spend time together that lights your fire?

Perhaps the **words of affirmation** they say to you make you feel loved because the conversation is always pleasant. For example, they tell you things that agree with what you think and know about yourself. "You are the most wonderful man!" "The way you fix things around the house really is impressive!" "I appreciate who you are and how you love me!"

If you are in a new loving relationship, this activity will not be too difficult to do because everything your love does or says is perfect now. They could not possibly say or do more wonderful things, or be more amazing. No matter what, when someone is speaking your "love language," you will know beyond a shadow of a doubt what love feels like and why you do or don't feel it from those around you. I highly recommend reading or listening to *The Five Love Languages* by Gary Chapman, and the five points above are from his book.

It may also help you if you can think about what you personally like to do to show others love — not just this person, who is your object of attention, but in all your relationships. What do you do in other relationships and friendships that you enjoy doing or saying to show people that you love them? Look over the list and ask yourself "What do I do to show love?" When you get clear about who you are, and what you like doing for others, and then think about what you enjoy about what others do for you, you open yourself up to attracting more of what you want in all areas of your life.

Step 2. Once you have gained clarity about your *love language,* now it is time to ask your partner the same questions. They will probably enjoy this process since the two of you enjoy so much of each other. The conversation will be easy and both of you will feel the flow and delight in diving into what makes you both feel loved.

Step 3. Time To Get Playful! Now that the two of you are clear about what your love languages are, you can speak it to your partner and to yourself *every day.* It is important to remember that no one person can *make* us feel, be or do anything. It is only from a space of pure positive connection to our inner being that we feel joy, happiness, passion, love, appreciation, and complete confidence in knowing who we are.

When another expresses love in a way that vibrates in harmony with what your inner being knows to be true, you feel loved; when another person expresses words or acts that do not agree with your inner being, you feel discord. Feelings of fear and lack may come up when you feel separated from yourself. Being connected to your inner being and believing in yourself without being another person's object of attention will attract another who vibrates similarly, or believes this about you as well. This, of course, is not limited to personal partnerships, and your appreciation of and connection to yourself — the *you* you really are — will attract the best of all relationships into your reality.

The playful part in your relationship comes when you speak the language of love with your partner and, most of all, continue to practice it. Learning, knowing and becoming creative in the way you give and express love to those who inspire you can be one of the most fun games you will ever play. This playful, loving process will allow you the chance to play and make your moves on the one you love, through a space of constant appreciation. It will inspire your lover to continue to hold you as their object of appreciation and love as well.

Love feeds love. Appreciation feeds appreciation. The better your relationship with yourself is, the better your relationships with others will be, the better you will feel, and the more you will stay connected to your inner being. Continue to do this and your life will just get better and better!

Go Play Stop ~ The Playful Loving Relationship Game

Rule 1. Getting your game on: practice staying connected to your inner being every day! For example: You can do this by meditating, exercising, listing things you appreciate about yourself and others, listening to inspiring music, reading inspiring stories or watching inspiring movies — anything and everything you know to raise your vibration and allow your love to flow. Be "selfish" and give to yourself first and then you will have plenty to freely give to those around you.

Rule 2. Make your move: speak the love language of your partner every day or at least two times per week! For example:

If they enjoy it when you do acts of service, you can make them a yummy smoothie every day, or their favorite meals during the week.

Stopping everything you're doing and spending 5-10 minutes paying attention to your mate each day shows love to someone who enjoys quality time or gifts of presence.

For those who love physical touch, you can give them a shoulder or foot rub for 5-10 minutes right before going to bed or simply the next time you have a moment alone.

Say wonderful, loving words, affirming your mate's importance to you. If you appreciate something they do, notice it and verbalize it to them.

Get creative and make a fun game of finding new ways to express love to your lover.

When my husband and I were first courting, we enjoyed hiking in the mountains. He would always surprise me by packing a thin blanket and bringing apples or other fresh fruits. When we reached the top of the mountain, he would lay out the blanket, we would share the fruit snack he brought and enjoy hours of conversation, lounging at the top of the mountain.

Those times felt magical to me and really fed our love. Other times, as I was at work, he would come by and leave notes on my car. I still surprise him at work by bringing him lunch when he least expects it, dressed up in a sexy short skirt. His love language is words of affirmation and I love to text him sweet notes and let him know how much I appreciate all the abundance he brings into our family.

There are many ways for all of us to surprise, excite and show love to our sweethearts, and when we do, they feel loved and express love back to us. Showing love in fun and playful ways will give you the opportunity to expand your creative mind and you will reap the benefits of giving and receiving love in return. If you continue to do this, your partnership will last and your love with grow strong and brighter throughout the years.

When the Flame Burns Out

There may be times in your relationship when there are moments of negative contrast. Perhaps this has even become a habit or pattern in your current partnership. During these times, you may not feel like continuing to play the love game, or perhaps you even feel like giving up on your relationship altogether. These moments come when you have turned your attention away from what it is you *do* want towards that which you *do not* want.

Perhaps it all started when you felt disconnected, and that disconnection with yourself caused you to start seeing a "flaw" in your mate you had not noticed before. Before you are even aware of what you are doing, you begin looking for flaws in them. You begin to notice more and more things you are displeased with that your lover does or does not do, or says or does not say.

The more disconnected you become, the worse you feel, and within a short time you begin holding your mate in a space of lack and disallowing any well-being for yourself, your mate and your relationship. This is when you start to lose the playful love game. You may start to feel resentful and therefore stop speaking their love language. Your mate feels the discord and stops speaking your love language. The less the love game is played, the more the both of you experience discord throughout your relationship and elsewhere in your lives. Cars break down, someone gets sick, a financial crisis arises or any number of things show up to let you know you're not connected to the well-being of the real *you.*

Getting back on track and back in the game again can happen quickly and easily! Even though most of us have been taught that relationships and life, in general, are hard work, this is NOT the case. The only time life gets hard is when we believe it has to be hard. Yet in reality, life is completely easy and everything you want comes when you can change your perspective and point of focus.

Life Can be Easy

Nearly every woman in westernized societies is taught that giving birth is hard and that it is best to have your babies in a hospital, just in case there is an "emergency." However, I have found this to be another false belief spread around in our society. It is important to note that beliefs are **nothing more** than a thought we keep thinking, so why not change your thoughts and, therefore, change your beliefs and your experiences from hard to easy.

In 2001, I became pregnant with Carter, who would be my fifth child. As many mothers do while pregnant in this wonderful, technological age, I started searching and playing around on the internet, looking for new information and inspiration to support me through my pregnancy and the birth. Let me be clear here — what I stumbled on would become one of the most belief-changing experiences of my life, and **I am not necessarily advocating this practice.** I am simply telling you this story as an example of a changed belief system surrounding the birth of a baby.

At this point in my life, I had previously given birth to three children (Danyell, Marc and Breeana) in the standard American hospital environment, and had given birth to Mitchel at home with a Certified Midwife, who also became one of my closest friends. It was my intention up until this point to give birth to this baby at home with my midwife friend assisting, as the previous experience had been wonderful. However, once I read inspiring stories of women who had given birth unassisted with no more than their mate present, or at times purposefully alone, I was excited like never before.

I quickly went to Amazon and found four different books on the subject of unassisted birthing and ordered them all. It took me only a few weeks to devour all of them, which left me even more impassioned with a desire to birth this baby within the comfort of our home without anyone there except my mate. Looking back, I think what inspired me the most was that I was told I could **not** do this and the idea of doing it anyway felt empowering. I wanted to prove to the world and those around me how easy and perfectly natural it is for a very healthy woman at thirty years of age to give birth to a perfectly healthy baby.

After a month of information and inspiration download, I decided I was knowledgeable enough to share this idea with my husband. For purposes of this book, I will give you the G-rated version of what he said when I told him "We will be having our baby alone, just you and I. Doesn't that sound amazing?" His response was "Are you out of your **bleep** mind?!" No, I was not, but for three months Blake would have nothing to do with my crazy idea (so he thought). My midwife friend also shared in my husband's belief system and strongly encouraged me to reconsider.

Your Power to Change a Belief

For the next three months, I ignored all those who disagreed with me and instead continued to focus on my new belief by meditating about the joyful experience I wanted to have. Intuitively, I felt a very strong desire to change my diet, eating only fresh fruits and vegetables, all the time. I read more stories and experiences of other women and they became my support system. It is amazing when you make a firm decision to do something, like completely overhauling your relationship with yourself and others, you can create a burning desire to have it and you have no Plan B or any other alternative.

Somehow, I knew my husband would eventually come around. I just kept loving him and encouraging him to read the many examples and stories I was reading about. Two months later, the baby's due date came and went. I wanted so much for Blake to be a part of this journey, so I kept meditating and visualizing him agreeing and the two of us enjoying the birthing experience together.

Three weeks passed. I was still pregnant and Blake was still not on board. I started to realize that our baby wanted his/her own experience with his mom and dad together as much as I wanted this experience myself. Days before the birth of our baby, our family did a mild hike up Zion's National Park. I felt better than the four previous pregnancies, and I was just over three weeks past the baby's due date. On our ride home, Blake turned to me and said, "I will read some of the information you have presented to me and see how I feel after."

I was overjoyed inside! I just knew if he did the research and stayed away from fearful thoughts, he would support me and our baby would come. We arrived home and Blake disappeared into the bedroom with all the books and information I had been putting in a pile for him to read for the past few months. Within the hour, he emerged and said, "Let's have this baby! I agree with you! This is going to be a great experience!"

Within two days I went into labor, and after only four hours of labor, Carter easily emerged into the world into the hands of his father. When Carter came out, I could see he looked blue as the umbilical cord was wrapped around his neck three times. Without even thinking or feeling scared, I took him from his dad, who was in much distress from Carter's discoloration, and unwound the cord from around his neck. I felt as if I was being spiritually guided to take care of him. Next, I turned him over and placed him on my forearm as I massaged his back. Within moments, I could see his color turning pink, so I turned him over as his head lay in the palm of my hand and his body in my arms. It felt as if time stood still as I looked into his eyes and he looked back into mine and then did something I had never witnessed a newborn baby do — he smiled up at me, as if in appreciation and love beyond what any words could express.

Carter and I, along with Blake's loving assistance, had done something that had not been done for generations in either of our families — we had given birth at home, without assistance. Our baby was created by his mom and dad, and he was supported to come into this physical experience by his mom and dad. The experience forever changed me! I felt so empowered, I didn't sleep for days after. I wholeheartedly discovered that **a belief is only a belief until it isn't any longer.**

As I said before, I am not necessarily advocating this as the best or only method to give birth, simply illustrating how a strong belief can be changed. Blake and I had the opportunity to step back, become light and playful about the subject of giving birth and relearn the idea of it in a whole new way. We changed our thoughts and literally reinvented our beliefs about the birthing experience. Similarly, we can also relearn that relationships are easy by playing around with them, staying aware and moving in the direction we want to go, in a light and easy fashion. Carter came forth in an environment of love — music playing, people kissing and laughing, and into the arms of two people who believed in one another and their power to be a part of something which went beyond the beliefs of others.

Go Play Stop ~ Re-Light the Flame of Passion

The first step back from an unpleasant relationship or disagreeable experience within a relationship is to gain a new perspective and connect back to your inner being by remembering first and foremost who you really are! If there is anything you can learn from the experience of loving relationships — and of life — it's that **the power to change your life is within you!** No matter what circumstances are around you, you can choose and re-choose, and you are always free to feel better simply by adjusting *the thoughts you are thinking.*

Re-starting the Playful Love Game

Step 1. Who Are You? In a quiet space where you can think in, sit down and write a list of all your positive aspects. Remember stories you've heard of all the wonderful ways in which you add to the lives of others, including your lover's. Reconnect to *you* again. Become the object of your own attention and take slow, deep breaths, feeling the life and expansiveness within you.

Step 2. Once you are in a high vibrational, loving space again, begin to make a list of all the positive aspects of and things you appreciate about your partner. Remind yourself of all the fun and enjoyment you have shared in the past. When you hold another in complete appreciation, you hold yourself there, too.

Step 3. Now you are ready to start the Playful Love Game again and remember the *love language* of your partner. If you don't know the love language of your partner yet, figure it out. Ask them to remember a time when they felt the most loved by you. If this doesn't work, take one love language you think it may be and start to speak it daily for a week. Notice if you get a different response than normal; if not, try another. Continue this until you experience positive feedback from your efforts, then keep speaking it as often as you can. Eventually, your partner will feel the shift in your relationship and they will start expressing love to you as well.

Step 4. Make your move! Shine your love on your mate and begin to think of them in a state of complete love, speaking their *love language,* and be playful no matter what they do! You now know that no matter what, you are recreating your reality; the momentum of your thoughts, emotions and actions are paving or creating the future you want. The flame of your once-passionate relationship will reignite in time and even if they are not open to it, at the very least, you had fun giving love to yourself and your partner.

Another possibility is, if over the next 3-6 months your partner is not responsive to your affection, you will manifest a new, playful loving relationship by all your playful loving actions. This new relationship will be more of a match to the more playful, loving you and your current partner will easily flow out of your reality ***if they are*** not a match to your new loving vibration.

Remember, this is all a playful, fun game and love follows fun!

Creating Playful Loving Partnerships from Within — A Love Story

The night Blake and I met was one of the best nights of my life. We met at the airport working on the ground level, transferring bags from one airplane to the next or to the airport luggage pick-up point. I was a trainee and he was assigned to be my trainer.

It ended up being a slow night and for four hours of our shift we connected through conversation. I felt as if I had known him my whole life. He gave me his undivided attention and I gave him mine as well. He paid attention and when he saw I was cold, without me having to say a word, he took off his jacket and placed it around me.

As the night came to a close and I had to go back into the trainee class, I had forgotten to give him his jacket back. He came back to ask me for it, gently helped me out of the jacket, gave me a big, loving hug and we said our goodbyes. I walked back into the class and as clear as could be, I heard a voice coming from no one — I was definitely alone — which said, "You will marry this man."

The idea seemed perfect and I felt completely happy when thinking about marrying this man I had just met. The next second, I realized that he and I were both already married. The "married to this man" idea, then, seemed crazy and I brushed it off.

Over the next few months of working together, Blake and I naturally formed a beautiful friendship. Before we could help ourselves, we both realized how much we had fallen in love with one another. He had spent years in a loveless, disconnected relationship with his wife, no matter how much love and attention he gave to her. I, too, felt my relationship was distant and even though I had put all my love and attention into it over the past three years, it just seemed to be slipping away.

We were swept away and enjoying every aspect of one another and our love connection. Both of us had never felt this type of love before and we wanted to experience more. Ten-and-a-half months after meeting one another we became an official couple, moved in together, and eventually we were married and had two children together.

What you don't know from this story is how I created this relationship six months before I met Blake. It was around July of 1997 and I had just finished reading *Think and Grow Rich* by Napoleon Hill. This was the first book I read that opened me up to the concept that I create my own reality. I was excited and fascinated about the idea of thinking my way into the relationship I really wanted.

I sat down and wrote about the perfect partner I wanted to come into my life. As I was married at the time and having no real thoughts of leaving the relationship, I felt that I would either begin to notice these traits in my current partner or the experiment wouldn't work at all. Either way, I thought it was harmless to just dream up the ideal partner, write up a list, and then I packed the list away.

Six months later, I met Blake and six months after that, since my husband at the time and I had made the decision to separate, I was moving into my own condo. I was cleaning up a few things from my husband's house, when I found the list I had written, hidden away and completely forgotten about. As I read through the list, I started to think of Blake —

he was almost a perfect match to what I had thought about and written one year earlier.

For those of you who are not in a playful, loving relationship currently and would like one, rest assured that you are not left out of the Playful Loving Relationship game. Do you realize just how powerful you are to create the relationship you want, the life you want to live, and the person you wish to be? If we could all truly understand the power within us to create, we would understand our worthiness and the abundance in all things.

Creating amazing relationships is easy and fun! You might disagree with me if you have been in several relationships in the past that haven't worked out, or if you feel you have attracted several relationships but none of them turned out to be what you really wanted, no matter what you've tried. These experiences may cause you to harbor feelings of unworthiness or skepticism of ever attracting your perfect relationship.

No worries, because that was in the past and now you know how fun and easy life can be, right? Time to play more games and have fun attracting your perfect mate! The game of attracting an amazing relationship isn't much different than already being in a passionate loving relationship or rekindling a relationship you are already in. Each game of love and relationships begins with *you!*

Go Play Stop ~ Knowing Who to Attract

Step 1. Take some time in a quiet place to think happy thoughts and raise your vibration. Connect with Oneness in this state, thinking of and appreciating your elf. Think of your wonderful qualities and all you offer to those around you, whether it is in your friendships or family.

Start to list all of your qualities as if you were another person looking at you. If this seems too difficult, you can always think of the friendships and family members in your life you most enjoy and list their qualities instead. Think of at least 3-5 people in your circle and write at least 5-10 qualities of each person. When you are finished, go through the list and cross out their names and replace it with yours. The qualities we enjoy in others are also present in us as well — like attracts like.

Step 2. Now, describe on paper the perfect mate you would like to attract and fall in love with. Think of the things you would like to do with this person, the places you would like to go and the conversations you may have. "I would say _____ and she would say _____." I find that if you think of a setting like the beach or the mountains (or anywhere you like to go), you can more easily see yourself with this person. You will get a clearer sense of what they are like.

I love to imagine running on the beach with my love as we enjoying stimulating conversation. Afterwards, we are back at our large Maui home. I go in to get ready for the day as he creates a delicious smoothie for me. To surprise me, he meets me in the backyard and picks me up, placing me in a hammock under a shady tree. He lies down next to me, handing me my delicious smoothie, complete with a straw.

From my story, I know the qualities I want in a partner are:

Serve, athletic, strong, thoughtful, fun... and the list just gets longer, the more I imagine the scenario.

In addition, I can also create a scenario surrounding what I am doing, giving or being for him.

I imagine myself playing around with the water hose, squirting him as he begs me to stop. Then we head inside and I throw him down and give him a massage. He is so relaxed, he falls asleep and I head into the kitchen to make him dinner. He wakes up to a delicious fresh meal — a large salad and fresh orange juice.

From my story, I know the qualities I would have are:

Serving others, physically affectionate, enjoy making food, thoughtful, fun, and...

If you still need further focus to imagine your mate and what you would be like together, then it is time for you to get busy finding out more about yourself through various relationships. Understand that you will attract others who are like you. Focus on your strengths and amazing qualities and you will attract those within another as well, or attributes that will complement your qualities.

Go Play Stop ~ Mass Contrast

When I was young, I found it fun and inspirational to mass date. I would go on several dates just to understand more about the qualities I wanted to attract. Any qualities I didn't want to attract, I did not focus on. Making connections and sifting through the contrast within the dating experience can support you in designing your perfect relationship.

Go on many outings with a lot people. These don't have to be just one-on-one interactions and they don't have to be dates. As long as you are around all kinds of different people, including those already in relationships, you'll see lots of examples if you pay attention. Pretend you are a detective or a reporter heading out to investigate the best relationship for you and the qualities of the person you want to attract.

This is playful, fun and opens up your imagination to many possibilities. Once you have your list, focus on the love story you would write about you and your mate. Continue to imagine it as if it is already happening. The next thing you know, you won't even care if it is here yet, because you have imagined it to the point that it already feels real. Next, the universe will easily flow this amazing person to you and it will be even better than you imagined!

The New and Old of Relationships

Relationships are like us, as individuals — they expand, grow and change. In the beginning, love is magical and unlike anything we may have thought or felt before. Over time, the relationship changes as much as the people in the relationship expand and evolve.

It is natural to get what you wanted and then want more.

If at some point during a relationship, both parties are no longer expanding and growing on the same path, there will be a shift in the relationship. I used to believe that not all relationships were meant to last forever. Although some of this is true, what I found from my own relationships is they *are* forever — we just may not be physically together in the same space.

As my own relationship has changed with my husband and partner of 14 years, I am learning the difference between giving up and allowing. I love and adore this man; I have shared more joy and pain with him than with any other person so far in my life. We are renewing our relationship in such a way that even though we may eventually not live together, we will always have a loving, playful relationship.

We are all soul mates — connected in ways we can share. We cannot really understand another's perspective; however, we can seek to love and enjoy them from our own perspective. You have the opportunity in every relationship, and in every experience throughout life, to practice unconditional love.

Unconditional love happens when you can appreciate, love, and stay connected to who you really are in the face of who another is, how another is behaving, or in any circumstance that surrounds you. Unconditional love is freeing because you have the power to decide in each moment how you want to be, think and feel. Unconditional love is pure *freedom!*

The Best Relationships Start with Being Self "Centered" First

The best way to love and enjoy another is to first align with your inner being by raising your vibrational level. I find it interesting that some people believe that when anyone cares for him or herself first that it is a bad thing, that they are being "selfish." When you are truly *self-centered* — centered in yourself and who you really are — you have more love to

give, more love to share, and more love for others to experience simply from your example.

Wayne Dyer put it well when he said, "Until you attend to
your own trees, you won't have any juice to give away." Love
can be freely and easily given from a space of self-love. It is
quite ironic that our modern society teaches us to loathe
ourselves and love another, when in fact, that is completely
impossible. If you've unintentionally learned that, you'll have
to unlearn it and rediscover how to love and appreciate
yourself. The vibration and feeling of love comes when you
are connected to your inner being in alignment with passion,
appreciation, joy and love.

Remembering who you are first before you put yourself
last will allow you to play more, be more and love more! Stay
playful during your process of creating joyous, passionate
relationships and be self-centered.

Go Play Stop ~ More Relationship Play and Fun Ideas To Spark Up Your Night

You can turn any moment into a playful moment. Let
life be the foreplay to excite the passion between the two of
you. Play outside the bedroom to light the fire inside the bedroom. Think creatively and watch the playful passion ex-
plode.

Car Wash Play: The next time you're washing the car together turn it into water play. You can even plan to play by
inviting your lover to spend time with you out washing the
car. Within the perfect, completely spontaneous moment,
throw a little water their way. They will most likely do the
same until you both are drenched from playing in the water
together. After the car is clean, you can go inside for perhaps more wet and wild fun.

Dinner Time Play: While fixing dinner, ask your lover to join
you. Get your hands into the mix, like draining the noodles
with your hands together, kneading the dough or even standing closely, hip to hip, chopping the tomatoes or other ingredients. Toss the salad together with both of your hands and

play around with your food together. Come up behind your love and put your arms around them, caress them with their body next to yours. Simply your playful, loving attitude will lead to a feeling of intimacy and connection between the two of you. The next thing you know, you may be enjoying dinner in bed instead of at the table.

These are just two simple ways in which life between two lovers can be one big fore-playground full of moment-to-moment possibilities to create more loving playful connections. The main key is to start with the attitude that every day in every way there is always a playful opportunity. Enjoy every moment you can together and this will ultimately lead you to a deeper, stronger and longer-lasting playful, loving relationship!

7

LOVE WHAT YOU DO,
DO WHAT YOU LOVE

Why Play!
Play with your passion
and abundance will flow like rain!

Playful Surprises!

At the time I was the maintenance manager for a Bass Pro Shop. It was a fun, empowering job and I always looked for ways to bring value and enjoy what I was accomplishing for the store. On a few occasions, we had the responsibility of putting some NASCAR vehicles on display. Each time, I coordinated the load-in and placement as well as the display of the NASCAR show car and a Sprint car.

It was always a lot of fun! I got to know our truck drivers who delivered the cars so that I could coordinate load-in and load-out, and display while they were in my care. Usually we would push them into place, with the delivery driver steering through the driver's window.

One morning, the driver suggested that everyone else push, and that I climb inside and "drive" the car! As the car sat inside the trailer, I carefully walked down the wheel well and crawled inside the driver's side window. I positioned myself in the seat and then put the steering wheel in place. If you are unfamiliar with the inside of a race car, the steering wheel is locked into place after the driver is seated. It is kind of a tight fit. I steered while other associates gently pushed the car out of the trailer and into the store, until we reached our final position. It was such a fun experience! I sat in the seat that normally would hold Jamie McMurray!

While not everyone is employed somewhere that would facilitate that kind of experience, we all have the opportunity to have memorable experiences at work. Think of your interaction with other employees and your customers. I have found just a smile or the way I say "good morning" can make someone else's day. I engage in myself and in my work to have a more fulfilling day. I look for ways to make memorable experiences in my work life. I enjoy my life and my work. If I can no longer find a way to enjoy my work, then I know it is time to consider a change.

Pam Tyler

Be YOU!

Most of us have seen or been drawn to a person who is completely aligned in their passion. These people don't need to motivate themselves or others. They are clear, confident, passionate and charismatic naturally. A truly inspired, purpose- and passion-driven person can't wait to get up in the morning, "works" until all hours of the night, and seems to know how to make every moment feel perfect. They inspire us! They love what they do, do what they love, and know fully why they're doing what they're doing.

For as long as I can remember, I have been completely fascinated with charismatic, inspiring individuals who are aligned with their passion and purpose. We can all feel the difference between someone who is authentically being who they are and those that are unsure or afraid of who they are. Even though we may not have attained this level of self-awareness, confidence and purpose yet, we can't help but want it and even crave it. If you are not consciously aware of just how worthy, amazing and creative you are, then it's time you spent some quality time with you! You can get to know yourself more by focusing on your strengths, practicing appreciating and loving yourself and spending time with yourself. Before long, you will begin to realize your greatness.

We are all good enough — worthy enough — to have or be or experience whatever we want, but at times, we can be our own worst enemy and convince ourselves otherwise. From our own generated thoughts and beliefs, we think we have to do, be or have something in order to attain greatness. In my own constant search for personal greatness, I eventually realized I have always been perfect, and **you** are 100% perfect, too! All you "must" do is allow yourself to be you, *stop* caring/worrying about what others think, and stop conforming to what you think others want you to be. My friend reminded me the other day that "what others think of you is none of your business."

People who are dying often have regrets. One of the top five regrets is "I wish I'd had the courage to live a life true to myself and not the life others expected of me." The great news is you are still alive and now is your time, in this moment, in every second, to remember who you are. Shine, spread your wings and *be* your greatness — the amazing *you* we have all been waiting for you to be.

Passion and Greatness are Naturally You

I am one of those crazy individuals (I love being crazy) who likes to research others who are living their passion — those who inspire others just by being who they are naturally. There are many individuals creating huge ripple effects in their circles and in many cases around the world. Justin Bieber is a great example of such a person!

I watched the movie *Never Say Never*, which tells the story of how he became famous, along with various concert and pre-concert footage. Now to be honest, I have not listened to all of the music Justin sings but what truly inspires me about this young man is who he is and what he has allowed into his life. If you haven't seen *Never Say Never*, I highly recommend you see it, if only to witness how this young man was able to create his own fame and fortune through playing his passion.

From the beginning of Justin's life he was a star. He started playing music and singing from the time he developed muscle coordination. He felt passionate for something that excited him and he allowed himself to follow his passion and be who he wanted to be without a second guessing. Without riches and being raised by his single mother and grandparents, this little person knew, beyond a shadow of a doubt, what he loved, who he was, and why he wanted to perform in front of the world — to have fun, sing and entertain.

Through videos of himself singing and playing music on YouTube, a music agent saw Justin's passion and invited him to live the American Dream and be a star. After weeks, it wasn't working out the way the agent originally planned and none of the music producers thought he was ready for the big stage for at least another ten years. Justin wouldn't have any of their rejection. His passion, love of music and performing for others, along with his belief in himself, was stronger than any "no."

One day, after attempting to impress the popular music artist, Usher, with a cover of one of his songs, Justin just started singing without asking permission. Usher was so amazed by Justin's voice, he followed up with one of his own music contacts and thus Justin became an inspiring star who shares his passion with all his fans. This young man brings in the largest crowds of any performer and they all come for the experience of who he is and who he knows himself to be.

This is just one of many inspiring stories of people who play their work, doing exactly what lights the fire of passion within their soul. People like Lance Armstrong, Oprah Winfrey, and Michael Bublé, do what they love, love what they do, and are so clear about this, they naturally inspire others to follow and create a path of wealth as well.

Different is Playfully Good

From the time I was 11 years old, I knew I would eventually do something different and unique in the world. After all, I couldn't be weird, different, crazy and playful just for fun, right? For years, I didn't embrace who I was, and instead I tried to be like others and fit into boxes created by others. The more I tried to conform, like many of us do, the more I became unhappy, frustrated and angry with myself and my life.

What I finally realized is that my constant playful spirit, my child-like ways, my uniqueness and different way of thinking were not my weaknesses after all. They were my greatest assets and what inspired others who did enjoy being around me. Your excellence can come from the traits and qualities others may tell you are your faults, annoying habits, or differences that set you apart from the crowd; these are really your assets.

Einstein was told he was dumb and would never amount to anything by his teachers in school. Luckily, neither he nor his parents believed this and he went on to be one of the greatest minds in history. His unique learning style supported him in thinking outside the box — way outside the box.

Daniel Pink, the writer of *A Whole New Mind*, has done extensive research on the new era called the Conceptual Age. In the Conceptual Age, a person with **a whole new mind** thinks outside the box in creative and empathic ways. It is now extremely important to use the right side of the brain, or the creative part of us, that is just waiting to emerge after being pushed down, ignored and considered unimportant. Unless, like a few, you managed to stay in touch with your artistic nature (despite the bad rap), now, more than ever, it is time for each of us to reunite with our artistic side.

Daniel suggests that, with the development of Asia, automation and abundance, in order to truly compete and succeed now, we all need to combine our own creativity and empathy through six essential senses:

- Design (engaging the senses)
- Story (tell a story surrounding your products and/or services)
- Symphony (innovative, big picture thinking)
- Empathy (beyond logic, engaging both emotion and intuition)
- Play (bring humor, fun and light-heartedness into your business and products)
- Meaning (the importance of the journey and the higher purpose).

There are so many more authors researching and sharing with us similar concepts including Gary Vaynerchuk, *Crush It*, Seth Godin, *Purple Cow*, and Simon Sinek, *Start With Why*. In fact, just take a look at the businesses that are thriving today, from shoe and socks companies like Zappos and Little Miss Matched, to restaurants like Pure Food and Wine and Aulac, and technology and programming like Apple and Amgen. These are just a few companies that are practicing this out of the box — or *play* with the box — way of doing business, and they're succeeding financially, in team creation among their employees, and at the same time making a difference in the world.

Think about your own unique gifts, strengths and talents. It no longer matters what qualities others have — what does matter is what you personally have. Henry Ford was famous for saying, "Whether you think that you can, or that you can't, you are right." You have the ability to achieve any level of greatness, no matter how small or large. It is your belief in yourself and what you have to offer and create that will make all the difference.

So, whether you're dyslexic, short, tall, have the ability to write or speak well, or possess the skills or know-how you think you need, hear this: there is really nothing you need to learn, do or be in order to be successful in whatever you choose to do **except** to take the first step that feels good, then the next, and the next, until you arrive at your destination. You have all you need within you now, you were born ready and through your life experiences, both good and bad, you have refined yourself even further. Justin Bieber never had a day of voice lessons until he became a star. The Beatles were not originally the best musicians — they loved to play music and practiced by playing for hours "7 days a week", and Taylor Swift was discovered while singing her songs in a restaurant.

Who knows what path you will be led to, and what passion will boil up from within you when you believe in and love yourself completely. Imagine the possibilities of a life full of joy, passion and purpose — a life where what you do to bring in abundance is what you would do no matter what. Playing around with your differences, your abilities and your uniqueness will take you places you may have never thought to go before. Being different, crazy, strange and weird (any of those qualities) is actually cool, attractive and marketable.

Play Your Passion and Success Follows

In the beginning, when I first received the inspiration to create a Play Movement, including this playful book, I thought it was a crazy, too-simple idea nobody would be interested in. At first, I couldn't imagine myself leading and inspiring adults to play — I wasn't even sure people would want or need someone to encourage them to add play and fun back into their lives. I decided in order to understand this whole play idea I kept receiving inspiration about, I would do some research to see if people wanted to play. I began to ask others what they thought about play and how much they were already playing and having fun in their lives.

When I asked children and young people what they thought of adults they said, "Adults are boring and uptight all the time." Then, I really knew I was onto something when I was listening to a recording of a *grown-up* conference when a 12-year-old boy was chosen from the audience to ask the speaker a question, "Why are adults always so angry?" Another day, I read an article about regrets people had just before dying. Many said, "I wish I had played more and worked less." My first thought after reading this was, "Can't we do both? Let our work be our play and our play be our work?"

For several days, I had opportunities to talk to both close friends and strangers and ask them questions surrounding play. Looking back, I didn't know just how much I was already inspiring those around me to play, have fun and feel joyful in spite of any "negative" contrast they were experiencing in their lives. In addition, I didn't notice how many people, beyond their younger years, are no longer playing just to have **fun**. My friends and I who continued to play *just to play*, were, unfortunately, the minority. Many people expressed regret because at some point they were told to "grow up" and/or "stop playing around" and because they were told this so often, they eventually did.

After about a week of my playful "research," I concluded that indeed many adults have forgotten about their playful spirit. Most have buried their playful self deep inside and, from their excited expression at the mention of playing, I'd say they are ready to reunite with it and remember to play again. This was more than exciting — this was monumental! For years, I wanted more than anything in the world to inspire others in a huge way. The only problem was I didn't know what my passion was and what I was to inspire others to do.

Unlike me, you may already know your passion and if you're not already pursuing it, it's about time you start. Believe in yourself! "Just do it!" No matter what your current circumstances are, be sure you don't, as Wayne Dyer says, "die with your music still in you." Only you have the power to change your life, to do what you love and love what you do. You don't have to know how you're going to be a famous singer, just sing. You don't have to know how to be a comedian, just get up in front of people and tell your funny stories and jokes.

It is not the *how you do what you do* that will be bring you success but the *why* — the passionate feeling you get when you are doing what you love. Having fun and being passionate are contagious and everyone wants to be a part of the excitement. You never need to know all the answers, because when you are completely passionate and having an amazing time doing whatever it is you love to do, success will naturally follow you!

Go Play Stop ~ Clueless, What's my Passion?

I completely understand if you don't know yet what you are passionate about or feel inspired to do. For me, playing is what I have always naturally done, but I didn't realize it was worth pursuing as a passionate career until I started researching. I love more than anything to throw parties for others, take trips with them, or play around doing just about anything. I even play while I am running — I have so much fun and feel so good running that often I bust out dancing. My point is that what I was naturally passionate about was right in front of my nose the whole time; I just had to believe in myself in order to see it.

Uncovering your passion isn't as difficult as many people make it out to be. There are several books on the subject of finding, creating or discovering your passion, but there are a few basic **fun**damentals that are "key" to recognizing a talent, passion or love you already have and may not be aware of.

Step 1: Love Yourself. Throughout this book, I write about radical self love or self-centered love over and over because this is the most important element in any part of life. You simply must learn to really love yourself because guess what? You are stuck with you. No matter where you go and what you do, you will always take *you* along with you.

If your relationships are not working, it is because you are not in alignment with who you are. Whoever you are having problems with is simply a mirror for you (remember chapter 6?). These mirrors give you the opportunity — believe me when I say "give you the opportunity" — to know yourself more. When you align with your inner being, your relationships will improve too. It all starts with you first and foremost!

Let me illustrate. For years I had a "problem" with the way my parents treated me. I felt they continually disapproved of me, and they expressed themselves using phrases like, "you are so difficult! Why can't you be like other kids? I don't understand you!" The more I thought of myself as difficult and different in a bad way, the more they re-enforced this thought with their words and behavior towards me. This continued into my adult years, worsening and carrying over into my relationships with my siblings.

Dr. Wayne Dyer says "When you change the way you look at things, the things you look at change." After hearing and finally understanding the meaning behind that piece of wisdom, I was able to change my environment with my family by changing my perspective about myself. For months, I really worked on my thoughts about myself and began to see myself in a whole new, loving perspective.

This completely changed my outlook on me, my life and my family. No longer was I the victim of my life but the creator and the victor. My family was only reacting or responding to my own beliefs about myself. With my alignment to my inner being and renewed self love, I was able to see my childhood in a new light. What I once viewed as a "terrible" experience growing up became wonderful and amazing, full of growth and facilitating the expansion into the amazing person I am today.

My siblings started to respond differently to me and our relationships are changing — becoming more loving and connected. At my mom's funeral, I realized how proud I am to be like her. As each person came to offer their condolences, they each expressed stories of fun and playful experiences they had with my mom. I felt my heart fill with pride and love as I finally realized just how amazing she was and how much I am like her. She was, as I am, a naturally playful person! In the past I failed to see it, but now, because

I changed the way I looked at myself (and her), I could see her playfulness clearly.

🛑 *Go Play Stop ~ Open up, Expand and Let the Inspiration Flow*

1. On a large piece of paper, make two columns and at the top of one side write **Problems** and on the other side write **Gifts**. Now, write down the person or people you have a "problem" with, whether it's your family members, friends, or others in your life. Write a few points or a quick sentence to summarize the problem(s); feel free to judge them as harshly as you wish.

Go through each name and with your pen, cross out each person's name and write your name above their crossed-out name.

Your power comes when you understand that these problems are *yours.* Example: When I start to reprimand my children for not picking up after themselves, I stop. As the words come to mind, I look around and realize I have not been picking up after myself either.

Fix your problems and others will, too. By taking steps to correct the problems you have with-others-within-yourself, you will stop seeing those problems in others or they will just "magically" go away. Example: I didn't like how my daughter would bite her nails so low they would bleed. I realized I too was biting my nails. When I stopped, so did she and I never said a word to her.

The only space you have power in is your space. The people around you are a gift and they are there to offer you opportunities to both expand and to know yourself more. For a time, I thought my mom was the problem in my life — now I know she was my biggest mirror. She was always showing me my potential and what I could work on, or play through, to grow and be more.

2. Fun Ideas! Now that you understand your "problems," let's move on to your gifts. If you don't yet recognize what your gifts, talents and strengths are, then, do the same process with the positive things you enjoy about those around you. Write down all the gifts, talents and things you admire in others, cross out their names and put yours above.

If you take a step back, you will see how you, too, have many of the talents and gifts of those you admire, or at least the potential for the talent. Example: I may not tell jokes or stories like my husband, the comedian, but I am goofy and funny naturally. Often, I make people laugh without trying.

Go through each "gift" you wrote down and ask yourself:

Could I see myself doing this in some way, shape or form?

How excited do I feel when I think about doing this, on a scale of 1-10?

If I had all the money in the world, what would I do for fun and entertainment?

What would I do to inspire or be of service to others if I had all the time and money to do so?

Example: I could see myself entertaining others with fun stories that have humorous aspects to them. It excites me "around a 10" to see people laughing and being entertained. With or without all the money in the world, I would still love to entertain others.

Now think of a fun new way to utilize the talent, gift or strength that most excites you. Example: I am also interested in sports and have lots of stories about sports I could tell, maybe write about, that would have fun, humorous aspects to them. I could write a book of lighthearted, funny sports stories.

Try on Your Passion!

When you have completed this process, hopefully you will have a clearer idea of what you want and have some fun ideas you can play around with. These days, with the internet, Face Book, Twitter, blogs and YouTube, there are plenty of ways in which to try on your passion and play with it to see if it is something you truly love to do.

If you already have a hobby, would you like to turn it into

something more? Remember, the process above is there to help you to clear away any negative beliefs you may be holding onto, and to brainstorm ideas and recognize passions you already have. Once you try on a passion and take it for a test drive, you will find out more about yourself and what you like or dislike about your idea. Either way, at least you had fun and know more about what you do and do not like.

For years, I have been playing around with several different passionate ideas. In the past, I thought being a chef was my passion because I am so naturally talented when it comes to food. For a few years now, I have entertained people on YouTube with raw food videos and a free raw food recipe website called www.Raw-Food-Diet-Inspiration.com. As much as I loved creating videos and supporting people with fun, delicious and healthy recipes, I wanted something more than food alone to support others.

With the inspiration and passion I am pursuing now, I find myself so excited and overjoyed, I can hardly sleep! This is a thrill beyond anything I have ever felt — I know this is what it feels like when you truly meet your heart's passion. Everything about this aspect of my passion brings me joy and elation for living every day.

When you believe in yourself, love yourself and allow yourself to live from your passion, you will feel as if you are living in "heaven." You'll feel truly alive, with a craving for more, that carries you through life. You can't wait to "work" each day and feel as if it is life-giving to you and to others.

If you know what you're passionate about, start focusing, imagining and playing around with it in any way possible. The more you do, the more it will come true. If you are unsure of your passion, as I once was, keep playing around with anything and everything that looks or sounds fun to you. Try it on for fun, play with ideas and keep your eyes open for synchronicities appearing in your life. Most importantly, stay true to yourself and dream — dream the biggest dreams possible: of you loving your life, playing, and being happy and fulfilled, no matter what you are doing.

"Looking for a Job vs. Creating an Opportunity"

(Chris Gardner's *The Pursuit Of Happyness*)

In an economic recession (really, in any economy), it is time to stop looking for a *J-O-B* (**J**ust **O**ver **B**roke) and start creating an opportunity instead — an opportunity for you to thrive, expand and play with. Everyone has ideas. It's just the few that will actually start and, as Seth Godin says, *ship them.*

Look around you — there is always a need to fill, a space to play in, the ability to give others something, or a service people didn't even know they wanted but that they have been waiting for all along. Only you have the power, the connection and the niche to do it unlike any other person out there. And when you can take your most inspired idea and turn it into a purpose, a life-giving calling and a burning desire, you will move mountains and create something you never thought you could.

There is a cure for "excusitis" (making too many excuses) and it is called *play*. This is the magic, the fuel, for taking your life to the next level. You no longer have to be afraid to follow your idea, dream or purpose because now you live in the Land of Make Believe. Here all your dreams come true, your thoughts are things, and the Universe will bring forth all you will ever need or want in order to make it happen.

It is time to get off the train of broke, the track of lack, and the unemployment wagon — essentially, the idea of a "bad economy" — and start creating something fresh and new today. Play around with your idea until you feel so impassioned, so purpose-driven, that you can no longer contain yourself. When you do this, the Universe will begin to open up, expand and deliver everything that you need or want to "make" it happen, including more inspiring thoughts, people and circumstances to support you.

Now is the time — not tomorrow, not a week, month or year from today — to sit down with a pen and paper and start scripting out every thought, idea or dream you have ever had. It might help to think back to when you were a kid. Remember all the things you wanted or occupations you wanted to be, and figure out what you can give to others, do for others, and do better than anyone else. Loaded with your newfound vision, the world will open up and "magic" will start to happen.

Go Play Stop ~ Your Universal Assistant

Did you know that you don't have to do all the work for your amazing career or business to happen? You can allow the Universe to bring it to you. Oftentimes, we do not allow the Universe to bring forth everything we want into our physical reality. One of the ways we do this is by thinking we are in control and taking **action** in order to get what we want. We may over-think the desire and try to figure out all the details of **how** we will make it happen, when in reality, our only "job" is to ask for what we want, think thoughts that bring up positive emotions and do the next inspired thing, one step at a time. The Universe will take care of all the details and will do all the real work in bringing what we want directly to us.

After learning this many years ago, I thought about viewing the Universe as my own personal assistant. Having an amazing personal assistant is priceless — you tell them what you need or want and you have complete confidence that they will get the job done. You mellow out and relax, continuing to come up with more creative ideas, thoughts and feel-good emotions. When you have a Universal Assistant, your life is free flowing and your "work" (play) is to continue to experience life within all forms of contrast, as it gives you more creative ideas. Support your Universal Assistant by making *feeling good* your #1 priority no matter what.

I heard a very successful, wealthy man share a story about a time when he was in financial trouble with a large court battle in which all his assets were frozen. He told a friend that he was faced with needing large amounts of money to pay his bills for at least two months and didn't know how he was going to get it. He decided that instead of worrying about it he would go on the vacation he and his family had already planned. While on this vacation, he didn't fuss or worry about his monetary needs — he simply had fun, felt good and handed it over to the Universe. When he came back from his trip with his family, he received a call from his attorney — his court case was dismissed and all his assets were released.

You have this same power within you because the Universe is always trying to give you everything — yes, *everything* — you want, need, and desire. The Universe is abundant, expansive and sees you as deserving of it all. When you can let go of your belief that it is your job to make it all happen, or that you need to earn it somehow, you achieve your own personal freedom.

Step #1: Replace your old belief that you must do all the work with a new belief that the Universe is your own personal assistant, and that you and It are in a loving partnership. You can start this process by continually remembering that you are the creator of your own life experience — through thought, not action. Everything from the children or family you have and the house you live in, to the divorce, speeding tickets and expensive repairs you have, were all created by you.

I talk about "remembering" because there was a time before you entered your body when you clearly understood that you are the creator. If you take a few conscious moments to really look at your life, you will see how you truly are the creator. Think back to the thoughts you were thinking when you last had a negative experience. Have you ever had a trend of negative experiences happen after you have been in a cycle of negative feelings and thoughts? Can you think of a time in your life when you believed in yourself strongly and things seemed to go amazingly well for you? Through a bit of practice, you will start to really consciously see you are the creator of your life experience as it unfolds. This is a very powerful understanding, because once you believe this, you will be able to consciously create more of what you do want and less of what you don't.

Step #2: Understand your part in the creative process. It is vitally important that you take your job seriously: feel good no matter what and as much as possible. I know that this sounds like a simple and hard job all at the same time. This is why I am writing this book about play. When you can look at life through the eyes of your playful self, you see life with a whole new perspective. Play is a fun and feel-good distraction to negative thoughts that don't feel good. When you find a way to play through a situation or take a vacation from it, everything will always work out to your advantage in the end.

This does not mean you will never experience negative emotions, but when you are used to living in a playful manner, you can let them flow through you without attaching to them. You are not your emotions, you simply *experience* emotions, but they are not a part of you. Your emotions are there *for* you, to help you to know more about what you want and they will determine the speed in which you will draw things, people and experiences into your life.

Emotions are the fuel in thought. When you allow yourself to focus on thoughts that feel good, like the excited, eager anticipation of a new car or house, and you can continue to feel excitement about it, you bring it to yourself quickly. The same is true if you feel angry about a fight you had with your spouse. If you focus on it strongly, the next thing you know, you're in another fight with your husband/wife or similar situation in which you feel angry again.

When you practice finding a way to feel good, joyful and playful most of the time, you end up creating experiences that will bring more joy. This is your only job — to live life, feeling good most of the time by thinking thoughts that make you excited and happy. Playing through your life brings joy!

Step #3: Let your Universal Assistant take care of the details. This is the hard part for those of you, like I used to be, who like to know about and control every detail. Looking back on my life, I can see how needing to be in control kept me from my desires. Remember the wealthy man who was in the dire financial situation? He did not worry about the "how." He believed beyond a doubt that the Universe would take care of all the details, and It did.

Now you get to let go and leave all the details to your own personal Universal Assistant and believe It will bring you everything in perfect order, timing and amazingly, even better than you asked for.

Doing what you love and loving what you do count in everything you do. When you can be happy, playful and find joy and bliss in each moment, you will attract more and more happy, fun and playful moments. Again remember, in every day and every way, there is always a way to play! **Play to live, play to feel good, play to let go of your worries and play just to be!**

8

The Gift of Contrast and the Comfort of Failure

Why Play!
Playing around with failure
will lead you to success!

Fun Exhaustion

We were all exhausted and at our wits end…that is to say, those lucky and talented few who had been hand-picked to open the new hotel were, anyway. There were about 200 of us in all and not a slacker among us. We were about one week away from the 'soft' opening of a 1500-room hotel that was to be marketed as the flag-ship for the hotel chain. Our job was to successfully set-up and "ready" for business the entire front office which included the front desk, bell services, valet parking, reservations, telephone operation, concierge, and reservations department. Yikes, what an undertaking!

My role was officially called Front Office Manager, but more importantly and accurately, I was the head cheer-leader! Late one evening after several long days of un-boxing and assembling massive quantities of computers, printers, office supplies, and the like, I noticed reams and reams of bubble wrap packing that had formed what appeared to be a sea of plastic bubbles covering the newly laid carpet.

"Now, what to do with all of this bubble-wrap?" I said to myself. These weren't teeny-tiny bubbles of bubble wrap; these were majorly huge bubbles of bubble wrap. I had an idea! I assigned a few tired and cranky folks the task of lining the corridor walls from ceiling to floor of the back office area with row after row of bubble wrap. They looked at me as if I was off my nut, which wasn't far off the mark as we were all pretty much emotionally and physically spent. They did it anyway.

I called a spur of the moment meeting. I told the entire crew to come gather in the back corridor for a short briefing...most weren't too pleased to be pulled off of their frantic assignments...but they did it anyway. I then proceeded to punch the walls. Punched the bubble wrapped walls. Popping bubbles...big bubbles make a very loud popping sound when you squish them. I invited them all to join in. We punched and punched and punched some more. We squished every last one of those bubbles. What a fabulous stress reliever...AND...it's much easier to dispose of deflated bubble wrap than fully inflated bubble wrap!

We all giggled and giggled. It was too much fun. After all the bubbles were squished, we all went back to work with a renewed sense of energy. What a blast!

Jan Dunnagan

The Gift of Negative Contrast

I have been sitting here in front of my computer for the past three hours playing around with music, Face Book and emailing my friends. You see, I feel the inner desire to write today, but just now, three hours later, am I finally getting the words out of me and into this computer. The problem has been that I feel as if I am in the midst of a bit of negative contrast. And as I write this book about play, I want to be in a fun, playful vibrational state — and yet three hours later, I am still "working" on raising my vibration to write playfully.

Finally, I heard a voice say, "just write." So, on the advice of Divine Inspiration, I am sharing my moment with you — I am sure you, too, have been in a position such as this, and may be clueless about where to go from here. How can we go from feeling despair, anger or frustration all the way up to feeling joy or bliss?

For years, I have heard about and believed in the Law of Attraction and the power within us to attract the things, people and situations we want, along with those we don't want. I also know that we are the creators of our life experiences and that we came into this time/space reality to grow, expand and experience life through both negative and positive contrast. Yet at times, when I am in the middle of the negative contrast, I resist letting go of the thoughts that are creating my negative emotions, and I resist seeking to understand the gift within the experience I've attracted.

This, of course, leads to more negative experiences of a similar nature and then more feelings of negativity, therefore leading to even more negative contrast experiences. Have you ever found yourself in this downward cycle? Ever ended up asking yourself questions like "Now what do I do? How did I let this person, situation or experience get the best of me? There has to be a way to stop this pattern I am in, but how?"

Next time you're in this downward spiral, take a Go Play Stop and seek out the *gift.*

Go Play Stop ~ Seeking out the Gift

I have always been the kind of person who wants to know more and expand my mind by seeking to understand everything I can about every situation and *how* I attracted it. When I attract the good stuff, I want to attract more of it, and when I attract the "bad stuff," I want to stop doing that. However, what I have found through my constant curiosity is this: You may not ever understand or figure out how you got to where you are, but you can still move on and through it.

The key is to let go of your need to understand everything, release the resistance, and think about what the person, situation or experience has caused you to want differently — or simply understand that this negative experience is all part of the plan the Universe has in store for you and that it truly is a gift. The only way we are going to know what we do want is by experiencing what we don't want. Think about the duality within life — we want peace because of war, we want love when we feel rejected, and we want to feel happy from our experience of feeling sad. Just writing and thinking about opposites excites me and my vibration is on the rise — how about yours?

For months, I tried to figure out what went so wrong in my marriage that my husband, after 13 years together, suddenly told me he no longer felt in-love with me and wanted us to go our separate ways. I felt more negative emotions from this experience than I wanted to. The thing is, after talking to him, I could see just how I had brought this on, as I, too, had questioned our love for years. Still, despite my personal doubts and feelings, I had stayed and done my best to keep us together.

I finally realized after months of tears and pain that it did not matter how or even why he felt what he felt; what did matter was the contrasting experiences in our relationship that had caused him and I to desire a new relationship. Looking back over the years with Blake, I found that there were many things I strongly desired to be different between us.

For example, the first few years together, we spent hours of quality time together, really being connected, talking, listening to one another and discussing our dreams. After our two boys were born, this completely changed and because he worked so much, he wanted to be home with our kids as much as possible. I understood this for years and even though I still wanted to spend time with him alone, I knew we had little ones and they were important as well.

As the kids grew up, I started asking him to take me out on a date and spend quality time alone with me. He didn't think taking me out was as important as being together as a family and continually dismissed the subject. Eventually, I started to take myself out on dates, but I still longed for the day he would want to go out with me again. The gift within the separation from my husband, and the contrast of him not spending quality time with me, has now created an even stronger desire within me — I can now see a future relationship to be one in which my sweetheart and I spend a lot of quality time together and he loves to take me out on dates.

By experiencing both the wonderful contrast of spending special time together with Blake and the negative contrast of no time together, I now know even more about myself and what I really do want. In this way, my marriage separation feels like a gift, as long as I continue to play around with my thoughts and seek out the gift within the negative contrast.

Rather than focus on what I am missing or losing in my dissolving marriage, I turn my attention toward what is to come and what I am gaining by not having this relationship. I think about and even make lists of appreciation about my husband and what the absence of the marriage has given me in my life. I appreciate him, because he inadvertently helped me learn where I have changed. Now that I am free from my marriage, I feel focused and free to create a relationship that is more in alignment with the expanded person I am today.

Take a moment to think about a negative situation, person or experience in the past that now, years or months later, caused you to have what you have today. Perhaps you once had a "fender bender" in a car that you really enjoyed driving, which made you sad; but looking back, that car pales in comparison to the fantastic car you drive today. Maybe you experienced heartbreak or a breakup that you never thought you would get over, and now, you can't imagine any relationship better than your current one.

If you take just a moment, get clear and even write down your contrasting experiences, you can really see how wonderful negative contrast is and what a gift it is as well. I bet if you, like me, play around with your contrast enough, you will begin to feel better and create more amazing experiences, therefore allowing more amazing people into your life. The more you play, the better you feel, and the more playful your life becomes.

Contrast and Failure

I like to think of contrast and failure as my playful, challenging friends. You know the friends I mean — the ones who push you, bother you or even upset you at times. You love them dearly, but often when you say something, they rebut, disagree or challenge you. They are really doing you a favor and giving you the opportunity to get clearer about what you want, see parts of yourself you may not have known existed, and come up with other ways in which to play with your life.

The majority of my relationships are perfectly flowing, fun and playful. I also have a couple of few wonderful friends who allow me to expand and grow in leaps and bounds because our relationship has a few major bumps and blocks. Without the contrasting experiences and failures how would things ever get better?

I have a strong belief that we are spiritual beings having a human experience and that we came into this time/space reality to expand. If life was always "sunshine and lollipops" and everything was always perfectly going our way without any contrast — or the opportunity to fail — how would we grow and expand? Seriously, how fun would life really be if everything were perfect all the time? I personally think that without duality, we might as well have just stayed in the spiritual realm or "heaven." Being a part of negative contrast makes this amazing life experience more exciting.

Whenever you're sick, you want to be well that much more, when your heart feels broken, you want the affection, love and attention of another even more, and when your bank account has a $0 balance, you want it full of money the most. The contrast within life can keep us focused and create stronger desires for what is really wanted.

Contrast and failure offer us insights into a more expanding world. The contrast allows us to "shoot off new rockets of desire," asking for more of what we want. This allows us to dive further into the experience of living, and learn more of what we can do and become. Failure drives us to succeed in new and creative ways. Making mistakes simply offers us the chance to know more about what we could do differently in order to achieve a different outcome in any area of our life.

The Comfort of Failure

What do I mean by the comfort of failure? I don't mean that failure is good, bad, right or wrong, but when you fail, you are really living life — and getting messy in the whole process allows us to go forward. Michael Jordan once said, "I failed over and over and over again in my life and that is why I succeed." You have probably heard the expression "to fail forward," but are you really listening?

A failure can happen in any game. When you start to play a game, you first learn the rules, either by reading them, from other players, or by figuring them out on your own. Next, you may want to learn the moves and strategies of others by playing with them over and over again— after all, we have other people in our life to support us. In the beginning, you may even lose the game, but eventually, you start to figure out new strategies and get better and better until you win. You may get tired of playing; perhaps you feel finished with a certain game so you go on to the next.

Life, business, love and relationships are the same way. In personal relationships, we generally learn the rules of a having a relationship by watching others, like our parents, in their relationships. In the relationship game, you may start by teasing or playing with those you're interested in while you're young. As you get older, you may start to flirt, date and get into lighthearted relationships for more experience.

With each new relationship and break-up, you experience new and different ways of being and interacting with others. You expand and grow, knowing more of what you prefer in a partner and what you don't prefer. You can never really master the game, because you will both continue to change and expand. At times, you may feel like you're finished with one relationship game and move on for the fresh new prospect of another.

The failures, or contrast, of past relationships have given you the opportunity to play the game differently. This time, you have the opportunity to attract another partner who is more your match as you have expanded from your previous relationships. You will enter a new relationship with more information, experience and strategies, to play a whole more delicious, fun and playful game.

The comfort of failure is in knowing that you are really *living life* — playing the game to the max, out there getting your hands dirty, and knowing you won't have any regrets when you're lying on your last bed.

Go Play Stop ~ Play with Failure

Is failure really to be feared and avoided, or embraced and loved? There is a belief out there that says "why try? I am going to fail anyways." If you take a closer look at failure, you may begin see the fun and playfulness within it. Many of the great leaders, inventors and creators of the past, present — and I'm sure it will be for those in the future — would agree with Thomas Edison who said "I failed my way to success!" He did not fail 1,000 times in his attempt to produce a light bulb, he simply figured out 1,000 ways *not* to make a light bulb!

Behind the basic feeling of failure, there is a playful drive to challenge yourself and keep going. If you can grasp this idea of viewing failure as a way to inspire you and peak your creative and natural drive, you may surprise yourself by what you can receive and create in return. For any greatness to occur, you must practice and at times fail — then instead of seeing it as a failure, refocus your attention on the possibilities that lie in the accomplishment of what you want to achieve. View the situation or experience not as a failure, but as clarification to come up with a fresh, new way of doing something.

In his book *Delivering Happiness*, Zappos' CEO Tony Hsieh discusses his many failed attempts at success, both in his youth as well as on his road to success at Zappos. What truly inspires me about Tony is his drive to figure out a new way of doing business, creating a playfully fun employee culture which ultimately leads to his employees providing excellent customer service. At one point, when the company was on the verge of "failure," he continued to inspire those around him, even to the degree that in the beginning his employees were working for free and living in his former party loft.

He held a strong belief in his company, his passion, and himself to move forward, face failure and continue to stay true to his heart — regardless of the "bottom line." His continual focus to follow his heart lead to Zappos' reaching a billion dollars in sales in only eight years and today, Zappos is even more successful. Tony understands the power to inspire and believe in others as much as he believes in himself.

Tony really played the game of life, took risks and became comfortable with failure. He got out there in the world and got messy gaining more experience in the game, through the contrast of his previous life experiences and failures. In reality, you can never really fail, or "be a failure," but you can prevent your success and well-beingness.

When you don't feel as if your life is flowing well, it is because you are standing in the way of letting it be. Like a dam in the middle of a river that prevents the flow of water, we too create our own dams, thinking they are for our own good. Our dams are fear, anger, and resentment, and may also include: closing ourselves off to love, forcing or trying to control ourselves or others, doing things we just don't want to do, or continually thinking thoughts and creating beliefs that we are less than worthy.

I want you to hear this message as if I am proclaiming it loudly inside your head: "You are **amazing** and **worthy** of **anything** and **everything**, but most of all, you are more than

worthy to be **joyful**, **loved** and **have anything your heart desires**!" There is nothing you need to do, be or have to make you better or more worthy, *you just are*. It does not matter how many times you fail, trip, fall or do something you are not proud of, you get to wake up, start over and you are worthy still.

Once you can allow the worthiness of who you are to shine through and know there is nothing that you can fail at, there is nothing that you will not have in your life. Your own personal universe revolves around you and will continue to do so. Part of getting comfortable with failure is believing in yourself, and then continuing to fail or make mistakes. Be the inspiring leader in your life and play in the messy fun that awaits you.

No one ever achieved greatness by playing it safe and turning away from the contrast that comes into their life. Your "job" here on this planet is to play. You are on a spiritual vacation and having fun is what you're supposed to be doing. Sometimes the fun is heartbreak, business failures or people passing on, but that is all part of the game of life. If you will allow yourself to fall in love, even with the possibility of heartbreak, you will experience more love. If you allow yourself to start your own business, even with the possibly of a bumpy ride, it will lead to an even better business venture. After people pass away, more babies are born, bringing with them a fresh, new, expanded perspective.

Playful Possibilities with Contrast and Failure

Give yourself the exhilaration of living your life beyond anything you have lived before. Go out and get to know a new person every day. Go try on a new career, a new business venture you have always wanted, or buy a new, fun car. Trust in a stranger, your neighbor and yourself to always be there when you need. Bungee jump, sky dive, climb a mountain or open yourself up to love. The time is not tomorrow or the next day to get up on stage — do it now, today! Become friends with your fears, your failures, and with contrast. These are the presents you came here to open up and experience. Stay focused on the experiences you can dream up, experience all there is to life, and then leave a path of joyous expansion in your wake!

Go Play Stop ~ Successful Anticipation and a Burning Desire

The best part of an experience is at the beginning — the eager anticipation. Imagine how amazing it must have been for Thomas Edison when he only had a vision of what he wanted. How about Henry Ford, when for so long he had a dream of providing affordable cars for everyone. Haven't you had a dream that you wanted so completely, it felt so fantastic just to think of it?

I remember feeling so completely excited about the arrival of each of my children... and how amazing it was when I first fell in love with my husband and I couldn't wait until the next time we would see one another. The pure, positive, exhilarating *anticipation* of the idea was the thrilling part of the whole experience, and not just the "climax," so to speak. Everything you want and can imagine can become a reality just the same. With enough practice, you can eagerly anticipate your life experiences into being.

The best way to keep that positive feeling of eager anticipation alive is to create the amazing *burning desire* feeling. If your desire is for a fun and successful business and your last business failed, understand this was a blessing because the next one is going to be even better. Tony Hsieh had failures in the beginning of his business, but he stayed faithful to his vision, passion and burning desire for a successful, fun-loving company. Create your own mantras or sayings to inspire you and stir up that burning desire, perhaps something like "I can't believe how incredibly fun this new business is going to be when it's off the ground — so incredibly fun!"

Sit down, pull out your dreams of the past or present and write them down. Pick out the one that excites you the most, and come up with the most amazing ideas, story and thoughts surrounding this exhilarating dream. Play with it more and more — focus on just one dream at a time. The more you practice the thought of your dream with eager anticipation and excitement, the more the rest of your life with come into alignment as well.

A Playfully Balanced Life

True balance is not trying to take care of everything or everyone in your life but rather focusing, even playfully obsessing, on one positive thought or dream at a time. No matter what negative experiences come up, stay positively focused on and passionately playful about your dream. One great thing will lead to another and your life will only get better and better, and of course, more playfully fun!

9

PLAYFULLY SPIRITUAL

Why Play!
When you play,
you know all is perfect,
whole and great in the world!

Playful Spirituality Defined

Years ago, I used to think that being spiritual and religious was the same thing. Later, I discovered they are completely different. The difference between spirituality and religion is spirituality comes from a sense of connection you feel inside yourself whereas religion is based on "a specific fundamental set of beliefs and practices generally agreed upon by a number of persons or sects" (from dictionary.com). Religion is introduced from the outside — one must learn a religion — but spirituality comes from the inside — everyone is innately spiritual. One can be religious and not feel a sense of spirituality. Religion, in any form, works for some people and not for others, but spirituality is for everyone.

Some people are turned off by the idea of spirituality because they see it as unexciting, meditative, pretentious, perhaps even boring, or full of rules/beliefs similar to religion. I understand this perspective as I was raised within a very religious environment that I personally did not find inspiring. I was a child who enjoyed playing and having adventures, not sitting still and quieting my mind — I had no concept of that.

Even in my twenties when I was a fitness instructor teaching high intensity, adrenaline-rushing classes, my friends and colleagues would invite me to attend yoga classes and I kindly turned them down. Inside I was thinking about how boring it was, even though I had never experienced yoga before. Luckily, in my thirties, I was much more open to new experiences and finally allowed myself to experience yoga and meditation, and as a result, I became more consciously aware, spiritually connected and now, I completely enjoy both.

One of our biggest teachers of spirituality is Mother Nature. I personally appreciate living in a community so close to a patch of wild, untouched desert. Every day, I get to experience desert tortoises, snakes of various kinds, jackrabbits, quail and many other types of birds. There is abundance, presence and playfulness blossoming all around me.

One morning as I was peering out my window, I saw two small rabbits playing a game of tag together. Another day, I watched a mother quail scurry across the street first and then somehow, without making any sound, signal her babies to follow her. Just this morning as I was on my daily run, I was thrilled watching a flock of tiny birds flow, follow and play as they flew down to the earth for a brief second and back up in the sky again. There is flow and rhythm to the joy that abounds in these creatures — you can feel it in the air and energy around you.

Spirituality is beyond mere thought. It is a feeling — of connection, joy, abundance and playfulness. When you "get out of your head" and live from your heart, you are connected to the Source and stream of spirit that permeates everything and connects us all. Your free, playful spirit resides within the realm of spirituality. Where all the answers are, inspiration is, including everything you have ever wanted to be, do or have.

Basically, whenever you feel joy, bliss, empowerment, freedom, appreciation, love, passion, enthusiasm, eagerness, confidence, faith, knowing, happiness, optimism, playfulness or any other feeling that just feels good, you are completely connected to your inner being, your spirit. This is the practice of spirituality — feeling good.

Go Play Stop ~ Meditation and Thoughts That Feel Good

In addition to playfully connecting to your spirit by simply feeling good, another method to connect is through meditation. Now I know what you may be thinking, "How in the world can meditation be playful?" I used to think the same thing until I opened up my heart and closed off my mind in silence. Did you know that between the spaces of your breath there are inspiring messages just for you? All you need to do is turn off all the noise and chatter in your mind, then freely ask for the answers and inspiration you wish and be silent... listen. In this space, there is more to hear than any book, teacher or mentor could offer you, and it is customized for exactly for you. Isn't that fun?

Over the years, since I started my own meditation practice, I have learned more through my own inner guidance than in all the thousands of self-help books, spiritual books and various teachers I have listened to and followed. I have heard and deeply believe that each of us has a higher, innermost being within us. This being is unconditional love, knowing, enlightenment, and connection. Our inner being guides us through our emotions — when we are thinking something that is supportive or in our highest good, we experience positive emotions. This is an indication that our inner being agrees with us.

The opposite is true as well — when we are thinking about or doing something unsupportive for us that does not agree with our inner being, we experience negative emotions. Experiencing negative emotions like fear, anger and resentment also feels so bad because your inner being, who always loves and supports you, will **not** "join you" in your negative space, so you feel a separation between you and your inner being. You can reconnect by shifting towards supportive thoughts and then you begin to experience positive emotions again, and you are completely connected to your inner being.

Go Play Stop ~ Ask Yourself a Question

Here is a very simple way to see how this good feel-
ing/bad feeling communication system works. Ask
yourself a yes-no question and see how you feel — the feeling will be the answer. If you start with a tricky question that
you have a great deal of uncertainty about, it might be hard
to interpret your feeling. If you try an easier question, one
you know the answer to, you can sense how the feeling-
answer from your inner being feels.

Here is an example. My editor, Teresa, was trying to decide whether to take a part-time job. She was feeling very
undecided about it and having a hard time making the decision by thoughts alone. However, when she got out of her
head and into her heart and asked herself as this Go Play
Stop suggests, she still felt a mix of somewhat confusing
emotions. So, she asked herself a question she knows the
answer to is yes, in her case, "Should I do some knitting
later?" She loves to knit — it is one of her favorite ways to
play — so her inner being said *yes, definitely*! She sat for a
moment and focused on, or absorbed, how a "yes" feels.
Then, she asked a question she knew would be a "no" —
"Should I get back together with my ex-husband?" The reply:
No, no, absolutely not! It wasn't hard to absorb how that felt!
Then she asked herself about the job again, and tried to feel
the answer. It was leaning more towards "no," although it
wasn't as emphatic as before. She realized she could
probably take or leave the job, and either way, it would be
good. She could also try asking several more questions, like
"Is there a better job out there for me? Does this job support
me in my desire for personal growth?" This would help her
get clarification to the original answer.

This good-feeling/bad-feeling barometer can help you
make a decision, too. Simply breathe deeply a few times, sit
quietly and ask the question and wait to see how the answer
feels. You can do a yes-no calibration as Teresa did first to
get started.

There are also other various ways in which your inner

being will communicate with you. Perhaps instead of a feeling, you randomly hear a kind voice or song inside your head with the perfect message or lyrics, see amazing pictures or movies inside your mind's eye, or you just *know* — you can't explain how you know, you just *know*. Because there are multiple vibrations being emitted from you through your thoughts and emotions, and from others' thoughts and emotions as well, when you can silence your mind long enough, you have access to reading and receiving vibrations from within you and believe it or not, from others as well. At first, the idea of being able to read or interpret vibration seemed strange to me, but when I started meditating, I started hearing a loving voice that was unlike my own. This experience felt similar to all of a sudden speaking and reading a new language I had never heard or spoken before.

Receiving Inspiration

All great dreams and inspirations are given to us from the Source or inner being within us. Often this inspiration shows up in our imagination. You will know it is divine inspiration because the concepts, ideas or images you receive are "out of the blue," and you feel you can trust them because they feel good to you. You may have an idea you have never had before, or see a person in your mind interacting with you that you have never seen before. You may get an inspired idea to change something familiar and see more potential to expand upon it. Once this amazing gift of inspiration comes and a new idea is presented to you, you have the opportunity to dismiss it or continue to play with it and imagine it into reality.

During one of the most challenging periods of my life, I started to meditate for four or five hours a day, sometimes even eight hours, in order to keep the tears from streaming continuously. Meditation was the only way to escape my negative thoughts about my dissolving marriage as all I could seem to do was blame and even resent myself, playing over and over in my mind all the "wrong" or "bad" things I did to create this separation. Before this, I had never medi-ated more than 30 minutes a day, and even this was spo-radic.

As I laid there in the dark solitude, I practiced focusing on my breath and releasing any thoughts that came into my head about my current reality or past memories. After about one week of this practice of mediation, I heard a voice — a voice unlike my own — talking to me, and images of people and places I had never seen before started to appear in my mind.

There were images of people I had never met before playing, laughing, joyfully interacting, and there was a strong feeling of unconditional love in the room. The voice said to me, as clear as if I was having a conversation with you, "You are going through this so you can support and inspire others to play." Crazy…right? I thought *how is me crying and medi-tating going to help people to play?* The voice answered me, "If you listen and accept this inspiration, you will affect the lives of many and change the world." Then, I got an image of me on stage in front of many smiling, happy-to-be-alive peo-ple, and everyone was ramped up with excitement. I felt a sense of peace flood my body and heard "play will allow people to be one again."

I relate the story of my vision because I want to share with you how this playful book was written from an intuitive inspired or *in-spirit* space. This book, and the whole idea of play as a new way of living and being, was written and cre-ated for all to enjoy by simply listening and paying conscious attention to the intuitive inspiration I was receiving (and con-tinue to receive) every day. After listening and turning in-ward, I then trusted my intuition and acted from the inspira-tion.

Play, fun and inspiration come from the higher space within us all. We each have the opportunity, the choice, and the chance to hear, see, feel and even know without expla-nation, our own intuitive spirit flowing through us. When you pay (play) attention, or get silent enough, you will see, hear, feel or know all you want and need to. Being consciously aware, in tune with your intuition and receiving inspiration is only the first step — what follows after is all up to you.

For a time, I wasn't sure I felt worthy enough to share the inspiration of play as way for people to live their lives, but the voices and images never stopped. In fact, the voices became louder and the images just kept flowing in. I receive inspiration daily because I ask, pay attention, allow it to flow in and then take action. Inspiration comes easily when you release your resistance to it, be still, and be aware that it is inspiration especially designed for you.

There will always be a muse of inspiration to create works of art, a story of sadness or joy to sing or write about, or a brilliant new idea, if only you pay attention and allow the inspiration to flow forth. Life feels magical when you are in the space of allowing yourself to connect to the Source within you — either by silencing your thoughts or from thoughts or images that feel good and raise your vibrational level. This is all a part of Spirituality in its highest form, because when you believe in Spirit, the rest is so easy and freeing.

Go Play Stop ~ Your Meditation Garden

If you are not yet familiar with meditation, the most basic way to meditate is to comfortably sit or lie down in silence or with soft music playing in the background, clear your mind and focus on your breathing. If a thought comes in, just allow it to flow out. In the beginning of my meditative journey, I found a technique inspired by a friend of mine, Intuitive Counselor Erin Pavlina, which she called visiting Your Meditation Garden that still allows me to easily connect with my inner guidance.

In order to get to Your Meditation Garden, lie down or sit comfortably in a soft chair. Make sure it is a time when you can be alone and won't be disturbed. I've even done this after a yoga class in dead man's pose. Next, in your mind, create a staircase that you will walk up to your garden, with a doorway at the top. My staircase is a winding staircase and my door is large and wooden with a big, brass door knob, but you can imagine whatever you like.

Open the door, enter your garden and shut the door behind you. This is where the fun begins! Within your imaginary garden, create the trees, plants and, if you like, lush green grasses. My garden has beautiful tropical plants, a patch of lush, tall grass, one large oak tree and a large swing set with 2 swings. Find a spot in your garden to sit in a circle with your inner being, guides, angels or any other guidance figure you want to invite. Now, ask them for guidance and inspiration for anything you would like to know in your life.

As you are in this circle, surrounded by all this spiritual love and support, relax and quiet your mind as much as possible. While doing this, you may get a fresh new idea, a loving feeling, a verbal message of inspiration, or simply get a feeling of knowing all is well. When you feel complete, get up, send your guidance figures love and appreciation and leave your garden through the door and go down the staircase. When you feel refreshed, go ahead and slowly reenter your life.

After only a week of visiting my garden, amazing situations, people and experiences started coming into my life. You may want to pay attention to what the Universe begins to bring into your life. Out of all the meditative processes, this is my favorite. I have received lots of inspiring ideas in my garden.

Your meditation garden is great because it allows you to receive guidance from your inner being, guides, angels, or if you like, "God." It also allows you to release your thoughts easily until you get the hang of it — we tend to think so much, getting silent can actually be hard to do. The process of walking into your garden helps you make the transition from our busy world to a higher place. Your garden is a peaceful haven where you can be still and use your imagination to connect to your innermost self.

Your inner guidance is always communicating with you,

it is simply a matter of you being able to receive the communication and understand it. There are four basic intuitive abilities you can use to communicate with your inner guidance and the exact form each one takes is unique to you.

Seeing images, metaphors of something you may recognize, or movies in your mind's eye.

Hearing an inner loving voice that is wise and familiar to you alone and only you can hear. The sound can also be a song. If you receive a song, pay attention to the words as they may have a message and meaning especially for you.

A feeling or sensations in your body for example a "Yes" feeling can feel like goose bumps, tingles, butterflies in your stomach or any other good feeling you may experience in your body when you feel in-spirit and in alignment with that thought, person, or decision. The "No" can come in the form of a negative feeling or what some refer to as a "gut reaction". This occurs when what you are thinking or what another said or did that is out of alignment with your inner guidance happens. These feelings can come in the form of an upset stomach, ache in your "gut" or sharp pain in your stomach. In addition, there can also be a tightness in your chest or pain in your heart. (No wonder so many people in our society find themselves with stomach illness and heart related problems, these people continue to go against the flow of their intuitive guidance system.)

Inexplicable knowing

You just know something and feel confidence in the knowing. You may not even have an explanation about your knowing, you just KNOW.

Everyone has at least one intuitive, communication ability to receive the guidance and inspiration coming from within, and some people have a combination of two or more. If you are unclear about which intuitive modality works best for you, test each one out when you feel safe, secure and in tune. Your Meditation Garden is a great space to ask simple questions like "Does laughing feel good?" and then allow yourself to receive the answer through sight, sound, a feeling, a knowing or a combination of sorts. Once you have practiced simple questions, you can begin to ask bigger and more direct ones such as "What do I need to know most to live my life purpose?"

Go Play Stop ~ Playful Dream Land

Years ago, I read a study about the brains of children under the age of five. The article described how the brain of a person from birth to five years old functions like being in dream land all the time. As the tiny person ages, and his or her brain matures, the child begins to see the world as a reality and no longer as a dream. I was completely fascinated with this idea and thought it would be fun to view the world around me as a dream, like a child, rather than a reality.

Thinking from a dream perspective is fun because, as you know (since at some point in your life you have had a day dream or two!), you can do anything in a dream including changing the circumstances almost instantly. This Playful Dream Land is a land of lucid dreams, not the kind of dreams where you are out of control and just wondering what will happen next.

Let me explain more about how to do this to your greatest advantage using a scenario. I love fashion and dressing in fun dresses and, of course, shoes. The other day, I went shopping at a store in the mall. While in the store, I found some amazing wedge, platform heels and a beautiful fluffy dress. They were a perfect match and I wanted to buy them.

I love to play the Playful Dream Land game in stores. I pretend I am in a dream where I am a really famous and wealthy movie star. The staff of the store caters to all my needs and offers to start a dressing room for me. They show me all the latest and greatest styles and fashions. Oftentimes in "reality," a member of the staff does ask me if she can start a dressing room and take all the clothes I have in my arms.

I go into the dressing room and begin putting on the outfits I have picked out. Usually there is a full-length mirror outside the dressing room, and as I walk up and down in front of it, I imagine I am waltzing up and down the red carpet, complete with lights flashing from the cameras and reporters trying to interview me. Of course, this is all going on inside my head — if not, I may be escorted out of the store!

Lastly, I imagine myself handing them thousands of dollars cash for my fashions and leaving the store in my limo with an abundance of packages and boxes with my new wardrobe. The last time I did this, I won a $500 shopping spree at my favorite store. The power of the Universe is in your hands and if you play with life like a child does, you don't need to worry or even think about the "how." Amazing things happen when we just believe that they will.

Play around with your reality by dreaming yourself into a new, exciting life, full of adventure and drama. You could pretend you are like James Bond 007, Tinkerbell, or a famous movie star. Whatever you want appears, your wish is at your command, and in your imagination all dreams come true.

I use this Playful Dream Land process to inspire myself to remain present. Even though I am in a "dream land," I am solidly focusing on the present moment and it allows me to let go of the past or future.

Perspective from Spirit

Allowing your dreams, hopes and all of your life to manifest easily in the direction that feels good is all a part of perceiving life from a connected, spiritual perspective. Play around with your life; live consciously centered and more alive each day. When you take even just 15 minutes a day to be silent or visit Your Mediation Garden and connect with your inner being — your inner knowing — you have the opportunity to be inspired and guided beyond the physical world.

Each day we are free to make conscious choices about

everything, from what we eat to the thoughts that we think. We are already choosing our thoughts consciously or unconsciously and our physical reality is proof of what kind of thoughts we've been thinking. If you are not currently satisfied with your physical reality and experiences, then perhaps it may be time to take a Go Play Stop and connect to your inner guidance, or let go of your control and let your Universal Assistant handle the details.

This is your life and you get to create it and play it any way you choose. Napoleon Hill said in *Think and Grow Rich*: "Our minds become magnetized with the dominating thoughts we hold in our minds and these magnets attract to us the forces, the people, the circumstances of life which harmonize with the nature of our dominating thoughts." Our thoughts, emotions and beliefs are powerful and hold the key to attracting what we want to receive.

10

HEALTHY N' HAPPY
BODY N' BRAIN

Why Play!
Players feel, look, and glow with youth!

"We don't stop playing because we grow old; we grow old
because we stop playing."
—*George Bernard Shaw*

Did you know that feeling good and playing is actually *the* secret to the fountain of youth? Yes, through my research, I have found that feeling good emotionally will physically support your skin and muscle tone, activate more neurons throughout your brain, and cause your cells to reproduce properly. You may have heard that smiles use fewer muscles in your face than frowns, which keeps you looking youthful. Feeling good, joyful, self-confident, and having the best time ever, leaves you all-around healthier physically, mentally and emotionally.

Finding a way to play through your life and feel good now is the best thing you can do for the health of your body and brain. Imagine, if you will, all those trillions of cells dancing around in your body, sensing your playful feelings along with you. They react to your positive or negative feelings and thoughts. When you laugh, the energy and power of your laughter resonates throughout your physical being, sending out signals to produce more perfectly healthy cells.

The truth is there is no real "secret," magic pill, diet or exercise plan to health and an amazing physique alone, the practice of playing to feel good now is truly the "miracle" to a healthy body, mind and spirit. One of the really cool benefits of feeling good is that you're more likely to be physically active, eat better foods and think positive thoughts about yourself and your body. All this, in effect, produces more of the look, health and wellness you desire throughout your physical body and brain, as well as releases endorphins, causing you to have the energy to play more.

Feeling joyful, child-like and playful fuels you energetically. You naturally just want to run and jump around like a rabbit, climb trees, pick and eat fresh foods, exercise your brain by learning more and reproduce more healthy cells in the process. This is only the tip of the iceberg of all the ways a playful spirit can benefit your body, brain and overall physical wellness.

Playful Longevity

Have you noticed the physique and outward glow of a healthy personality? People with positive attitudes, no matter what their birth age, always seem to radiate youthfulness and a beauty that is beyond their skin. Playing not only supports us to feel good now, it also keeps us looking younger, too.

In John Robbins' book, *Healthy At 100*, he researched the young at heart — people around 100 years of age, in many different countries around the world. His research revealed that one of the primary causes of these centurions living so healthfully, being physically fit, and looking so youthful was their constant state of joy and playful nature. These mature adults were still able to physically and mentally participate well into their 80s, 90s and even early 100s in sexual relationships and leap around mountains at high altitudes as if they were children. Their health test results in all areas were off the charts.

These adults managed to remain youthful from their constant connection to one another, to their environment and, of course, to their inner being. Yes, they had to deal with the element of cold, or not having enough food at times, and other circumstances we don't normally experience in our westernized societies. The point is that regardless of their experiences or circumstances, they remained optimistic and light-hearted. We will all eventually die, or "croak," and leave this physical life, but we have the option to stay playful and young as long as we are here.

Play with Your Cells

For nearly the past 50 years of scientific research, scientists have tested and proven that our cells physically respond and react to our thoughts and emotions (see *The Biology Of Belief* by Bruce Lipton). When healthy, thriving cells are put into a negative environment, the cells became dis-eased and cancerous. Then, when the same cells are placed back into a loving, positive environment, they changed back into healthy cells again. These experiments were done using individual cells in a petri dish — just imagine what goes on in your body with trillions of cells every time we think and feel negative emotions.

It is no wonder that cancer and diabetes are on the rise in many societies where feeling joyful and happy are the exception and not the rule. In cultures where the physically healthy and happy aging adults live, diseases like cancer are almost non-existent. If your thoughts and emotions are predominately negative, then your cells react by altering their cell structure. Over time, as a person thinks thoughts and feels emotions that do not support his/her emotional wellness, the body continually responds by producing cells that match the emotions.

Louise Hay has demonstrated the power of loving and forgiving yourself and others, in her book "You Can Heal Your Life". Even Louise herself healed her own cancer without medical support through the practice of love, understanding and forgiveness. She and others have proven that diseases, like cancer, are not really diseases of the body but a physical manifestation of the emotional dis-ease of a person's thoughts and emotions. When a person can shift their thoughts in a playful direction, their physical as well as their emotional wellness improves. Your physical health is only an indicator of the thoughts and emotions you have continued to practice and given attention to.

For instance, if you stand in front of the mirror and constantly think that you are fat and feel bad about it, your body and cells respond by keeping you at your current figure or by adding on more fat. Then, no matter what diet you eat, you still tend to gain weight, or lose it and gain it back again, because your negative thoughts never changed. I have several friends and family members who have even gone so far as to have parts of their stomach removed to lose weight. Within a short time, they gained it all back or created new health problems in place of their body fat. If the negative thoughts and emotions about themselves were instead "cut out," then they would never need surgery and would easily and naturally release the weight.

In order to alter your body and fat cells, the work — or rather play — is not necessarily in controlling the food you consume or the physical exercise you do (although both are important, too), it is more in changing the thoughts you think about yourself. You become what you think! So whether you would like to change the look of your body or your physical health, with a playful approach, you can easily raise your vibration and focus yourself into being fit and healthy.

Another illustration of this comes from the movie, *The Secret*. One of the guests in *The Secret* is a woman who was once diagnosed with cancer. Instead of taking the medical approach, she chose to focus her thoughts on her wellness and eliminated the cancer naturally. This woman consciously changed her diseased cells through laughter, fun and continuous appreciation for her healthy body. She imagined she was already well and healed; her thoughts and feel-good emotions changed her physically and within a few short months, her cancer was gone.

Think of how adding a playful mindset will change your health, your physical appearance and even your brain. Because our bodies are always in a state of reproduction — new cells replacing the old — your positive thoughts and emotions can heal you quicker than the illness was created. Simply by shifting to a playful perspective, you will be restructuring your cells from the inside out. Your eyes will become brighter, your step a little higher, and your body a bit lighter, all from your playful attitude.

Playful Escape

In the world we live in today, so many individuals are constantly trying to escape the pain of "reality" or the pain within their body through the use of various forms of drugs, junk foods, shopping, sex, television, and the list goes on. I've been there, too; I was on this self-destructive path when I was young and experimenting with various forms of drugs. It amazes me now that I, or anyone else, would want to "escape" this wonderful world we live in, when instead we could simply choose to play through our life to feel naturally high and healthy.

Our time/space reality offers us so much to be desired — to be a part of — and we are always free to shift our focus and heal our bodies, solve our emotional problems and even expand our minds. We can do all of this and more without the use of stimulants and unsupportive distractions, which only offer us a temporary escape that, eventually, we must rely on in order to briefly feel good. We become addicted to the fix, when instead, we have the opportunity to experience a high beyond what drugs or external, unhealthy distractions can offer us. That high is the magic of conscious creation found within you.

Once you utilize the power within you to create your reality on purpose, you will know there is nothing better than when you can practice the vibration of pure, positive alignment with the being you really are. Your life will become full of all the right people, experiences, health and the pure joy of just being alive. You have the power *now,* in this physical moment, to change the direction of your health, your body or anything you wish toward what you want.

Health and Wellness are Priceless

Health and wellness are free — you don't have to pay anything to anyone to experience everything you have ever wanted. When you feel good emotionally, all good things come your way — and that includes amazing health and the body you have always wanted but never believed you could have. Playful supportive distractions are healthy and they don't cost a penny; simply play around with your imagination and imagine your new, fit body into being.

When your physical wellness is in alignment, you feel more able to do any fun thing you want to do — bungee jumping, anyone? — or keep up with your kids and have energy left over, and ultimately dream bigger and better dreams. Health and your physical appearance are created first through your thoughts and emotions, and then they manifest physically. If you want to be, do or have something — anything — including the best health and a body money can't buy, you have to consciously create the vision first. You can do this entirely in your imagination, or you can make a vision board to help you. You can even tell yourself stories about how fantastic it is to have perfect health and a great-looking body, and the fun things you get to do with your awesome muscles and energy level. As with other visualizing, imagine your health as if it is already here, and refuse to focus on anything else.

Imaginary distractions are great, but sometimes you might not be quite able to fool yourself. If you can't find a way to feel good about your body or your health yet, focus your attention on something else in your life you *can* naturally and easily play with to feel good now. Thinking thoughts that cause you to feel playfully good as many of your waking hours as possible is the best medicine you can take — you can always rely on it, there are no nasty side effects, and it is free!

Go Play Stop ~ Playing with Your Food

Now let's get busy and play your way to health and wellness by playing with your food. Yes, I know that your loving mother, father or grandparent in an attempt to get you to exhibit "good manners" told you not to play with your food. I am going to discredit the whole "good manners" establishment and say that playing with your food is not only fun, it is good for your body, too!

If you were to come over to my house on any given day, you could witness two school-age children playing around in the kitchen with various fresh fruits, vegetables, leafy greens, seeds and nuts. Without a hot stove, oven or microwave, these two fun beings will blend, mix, or create something for you so yummy, you will think eating good-for-you food is more of an art form than a chore. I am talking about the two youngest children who came out of my body, Mitchel and Carter.

These boys are two of the healthiest, fun-loving, playful people I know. They enjoy playing with their food to such a degree that they inspire others to eat more fresh foods just by watching them. Mitchel takes meticulous time and attention in slicing and dicing all the fresh ingredients for each salad he creates. Carter is very particular about the measurements and amount of ingredients he tosses and combines in a bowl. They, like you, are completely creative beings and they love to express their creativity in the kitchen.

I once asked an intuitive counselor what my business niche was. She said, "you bring joy, playfulness and sexiness to something that people dread, like diet, exercise and eating better." My wish for this entire book is to bring joyful, playful and perhaps a few sexy ideas to support you in feeling good by playing through your life. Playing with your food and with the idea that eating healthy can actually be fun and delicious is just one of the ways in which I want to inspire you.

When you are open and ready to play with your food, start by washing your hands, rolling up your sleeves and creating a marvel of art. Take out an avocado, an orange, your favorite seasonings, any of your favorite non-sweet fruits like red bell peppers or tomatoes and a head of lettuce. You can cut the avocado or simply press on the outside of the peel and break it open with your fingers. No need to worry if your hands get messy — this is all part of getting your DNA into the mix as you are predigesting the food first with your hands and fingers.

Next, open the orange and squeeze all the juice on top of the avocado and then sprinkle it on top of your favorite seasonings like dill or thyme. With your hands and fingers (or a fork) mash it all together to create your tasty new dressing. If you don't like avocado, you can use mango or any kind of nut or seed butter instead.

Chopping, dicing or just throwing in the vegetables and non-sweet fruits can be done in many creative ways. Play with your veggies by slicing them into fun shapes, sizes, or even create flowers. Lastly, break or slice up the lettuce and toss it all together, making sure to use your hands. This can be especially fun with a lover and can turn dinner into more than just dinner, if you know what I mean. You can substitute fresh herbs, mixed baby greens and a variety of fresh, whole, nature-made foods to tantalize your palate.

What would dinner be without a dessert? Another way to play around with fresh foods is to come up with new ways to create your old favorites. From "Mom's apple pie" to creamy, dreamy, chocolate shakes, there are so many fun and freshly-made ideas you can come up with, if only you will put on your playful self, open up your imagination and get your creative groove a-going. For more fresh inspiration and play-ing-with-your-food ideas I invite you to visit www.Raw FoodInspiration.com. Make your life taste good by playing with your food.

Playing with Your Brain

Two very close, almost-sister friends of mine, who hap-pen to be twins, were faced with the reality that their mother had developed dementia and was slowly and continually becomes less the mother they knew. This contrast turned both of them in the direction of figuring out what they could do to keep their brains sharp and their neurons healthy. Many of the activities and foods that support the brain in functioning at its highest capacity include physical play, emotional wellness and fresh whole foods found in nature.

Other benefits of playing to feel good: your brain naturally stays alert, increases its capacity for learning, and you feel more inspired and drawn to healthier food choices. The more you think, read, play puzzle games and are physically active, the more you want and enjoy those things. The more you enjoy playing with and eating fresh foods, the more you will desire fresh foods. The more you think supportive, uplifting thoughts, the more you will feel good and the more good things will happen in your life.

Of course, brain exercises are not just for aging adults; they will also support those in their early years of growth and development. Fresh foods, brain games and feeling high on life naturally support anyone of any age. Test scores will increase, the mind's ability to learn increases, the mind gets quicker, and connects to others on a deeper level. If you start young, doing all these things will preserve your body, brain and overall health into your later years.

Go Play Stop ~ Brain Games

Physical Activity: Physical activity is a form of brain game and will support your body too. Playing any sport with or without others is the best way to keep both your body and mind active. Many have convinced themselves that they don't like to exercise, but if you make a game out of exercise or play a fun sport you are interested in, you will be playing and exercise won't seem like such a bummer.

My husband, Blake, is a naturally inspiring, playful person. A few years ago, he decided to coach our son's soccer team. He is the best coach because he finds such joy in children, loves to inspire them and loves to play games with them. This season, he had one of the best groups of boys he's ever had — almost every one of them was kind, caring (to one another as well as to players on the opposing teams), and they all loved playing soccer.

Blake had inspired in these young men a desire to make this a winning season by playing their best and improving on their best. During practices, he wanted them to run to increase their fitness and increase their speed. Some of the boys did not enjoy the running and would complain and ended up struggling to muster up the desire to run at all.

Being the playful person Blake is, he came up with a spur-of-the-moment idea to kick one of the balls clear across the field to the other side and have one of boys who did not like to run go get it. Then he challenged the rest of the boys to run after the boy who was running after the ball, saying "whoever reaches the ball first gets to choose his position." He made it a game and they forgot they were running.

He also found other ways to mix up the practices to make them more fun and enjoyable for the kids, like playing football, squirt gun war and hot potato soccer instead. Our team went on to be the only undefeated team in the league. At the end of the season, everyone was hugging and crying tears of joy. One child from the opposing team said to his father, "Why didn't my team get that excited and have fun like them?" The answer was that Blake inspired a willingness to play, have fun, connect to each other as a unified team and have a burning passion to really *play* soccer.

You can take any sport and make it fun and enjoyable for yourself and others. Over the past year, I have developed a love of running. After reading *Born To Run* by Christopher McDougall, I was completely inspired by the Tarahumara Indians of Mexico's deadly Copper Canyons. These people have mastered the joy and art of running. They party like it's 1999, or 2012, drinking corn beer and staying up all hours of the night, dancing and having the best time ever, and then in the morning, they take off and run continuously for days.

They are the fastest runners in the world and not only that — they love to do it. When you find something physically active you love to do, you will want to do it. Or you can be inspired to change something you aren't keen on, like running, into something you enjoy. I used to dread running, but after a few months of consciously looking for everything I appreciated about running, I began to love it more than any other physical activity.

Running feeds my soul. I appreciate being where I live and running in the mountains and nature that surrounds me. I enjoy expanding my mind and listening to books on my iPhone while running. My love of running has changed my body physically and my brain expands and fills with more information to support me further. You, too, can find a way to love and appreciate the exhilaration of physical movement to support your body and brain.

Reading: Reading is a game you get to play in your mind. The adventure, drama and excitement of a fiction novel can bring new ideas into your life, or the information and inspiration of a non-fiction book can expand your mind and offer you insights into more conscious living. Either way, you get the advantage of exercising your brain without even realizing it.

Puzzle Game: Some of my fondest memories with my grandmother were sitting at the kitchen table putting a puzzle together, or inviting my granddad to join us for a difficult card game. Playing any game where you have to figure things out or strategize will exercise your brain. You can play many fun games online, or on your phone or other digital device. The point is to have fun, and in the process, your mind expands and your brain gets the exercise it needs to stay focused and sharp.

Go Play Stop ~ Playful Purpose

No matter what you do, as long as you are having fun, you are purposefully playing. When you engage in play with others, you feel connected and your social skills advance as well. According to the research of Dr. Stuart Brown in his book entitled *Play*, it "shapes the brain, opens the imagination and invigorates the soul" and I completely agree. When we are playing and having fun, our brains are more completely open to learning and obtaining knowledge.

Every day, in every way, there is always an opportunity to create a playful experience to feel good, exercise your body, expand your mind and live healthier, longer, happier lives. If you really want to achieve health, wealth and happiness, then your sole objective in life must be to **feel good now**. Play is the best way to cause you to feel good, so turn anything you dread into something fun and enjoyable.

With your creative, playful spirit, you can find a myriad of paths and purposeful ways to have fun, enjoy every moment of your life experience, be healthy, love your body and use more brain capacity. I remember when I was about 11 years old, and I heard that scientists believed we use only 10-20% of our brain's ability. From that moment on, I have been on a mission to expand beyond my 20% (although modern research shows we actually do use all areas of our brains throughout the course of a day). The scientific and physical evidence also suggests that when we feel good, we can learn, do and be more.

I am personally hopeful that by consistently practicing our spiritual alignment to our inner being, we have the power to keep our brain healthy and have a more joyful life experience. Science now, more than ever, can prove that your thoughts and emotions affect everything from your physical health to the physical experiences and manifestations that you create.

Go Play Stop ~ Joyful Memories

Stop, if you will for a moment, and take a deep breath in through your nose and out through your mouth. Next place your hand on your heart, close your eyes and remember a favorite time in your life when you had the most fun, laughed the hardest and felt as if time "flew" by.

Got it? Now, really focus on and *relive the feeling* you had during this experience. Now imagine yourself feeling this way every day of your life. This is absolutely possible and when you do, you will feel and look better than anything you have ever dreamed.

The longer you can maintain the feeling of your past joyous, happy experiences, the more experiences like them you will continue to have in your future. You are a physically-focused conscious creator and everything you want can and will be yours! Play is the old and new way to feel good and create the health and wellness you desire and deserve most.

11

PLAY AROUND WITH YOUR VIBRATION

Why Play!
When you play,
you will vibrate your life
into being full of fun possibilities!

Vibration Is...

At times, it can be easy to forget that our physical reality is created through the transmission of our thoughts and emotions. For some of you, the concepts of vibration and the Law of Attraction may be new. Even those that are familiar with it, like me, still get caught up in unconscious creation and send out vibrational signals that are not wanted sometimes. The idea of our personal vibrational system can be difficult to grasp because often we want some sort of tangible proof that it exists.

It is often amusing to me that so many people, including some of my closest friends, struggle to understand that they are responsible for all they see and experience. Hardly anyone questions the idea of a radio frequency or of cell phone transmissions. We are taught about radio frequencies in school and in society, so we simply accept it without needing to know exactly how it works.

Personal vibrational frequency, on the other hand, is fairly new information now available to the masses. The truth is, whether you allow yourself to believe in thought vibration or not, you **are** creating (through your thoughts and emotions) the people, circumstances and events that come into your physical reality. "As you think, you vibrate. And it is your vibrational offering that equals your point of attraction. So, what you are thinking and what is coming back to you is always a vibrational match." (Abraham-Hicks)

Wouldn't you rather change your beliefs and purposely create the world you want, rather than the one you created unconsciously, and may not be enjoying? That is why play is so central to the Law of Attraction and your vibrational transmission — because when you are having fun playing, you will attract more and more playful, fun and enjoyable circumstances, events and people who match your playful vibration. To be playfully clear, the essence of playing *feels good* — it is a healthy distraction, and being a vibrational match to more playful experiences does sound rather delightful, doesn't it?

In reality, you don't have to understand the Law of Attraction or wrap your head around vibration. As long as you are feeling good, having fun or playing — which is something everyone has experienced as children — you will create a life of joy regardless of your beliefs. When you adopt a playful attitude and begin to look for ways to play, you will begin to naturally shift your vibration in a positive direction. With your new playful focus, in a short amount of time, your whole life will start to become more of what you want.

Vibration or Not, Just Play

I have a secret to share with you. Make sure you don't tell anyone who is opposed to the Law of Attraction or any form of creating their life consciously — "This book was created to get you, and those around you, to focus on fun and play so you can attract the life of your dreams." I know this is my own feeble, selfish attempt to get you to feel good now. Play is the best way to attract what you want, and when you are playing with others, it will help them to feel good and therefore attract what they want, too.

Now, in helping others, you don't have to explain the details of the Law of Attraction or becoming a vibrational match to what you want. Instead, just inspire them simply to feel good — with your playful spirit and by inviting them to play with you. Even if they resist in the beginning, in time I promise you that you will inspire them, because they won't be able to resist your playfulness forever. So start playing with your parents, kids, mate, friends or really anyone you meet. Every day, in every way, there is always an opportunity for a playful interaction.

Thought Vibrations

It is easy to tell how you are vibrating by how you emotionally feel. For example, suppose I feel angry at my mate because he was late coming home from work and I needed to leave for an important meeting. I feel angry and I am vibrating anger and essentially asking Source to please bring me anything — a person or situation — to further allow me to be angry. However, if I hold a thought about how much I enjoy being financially supported by my husband and am able to pursue my passion due in large part to his support, I feel so much love and appreciation for him. Now I am sending out a vibration of love and appreciation. Source answers my vibration and brings me more things, people and events to match love and appreciation.

Your vibration of joy, knowing, love or passion attracts more great stuff, experience, people and events to flow into your experience because you are asking Source to send you everything to match those good feelings. That's the magic key to unlocking all that you want, all that you are and all that stuff you have been ordering with your desires for all these years. Feel the good feelings and you will, in time, start to get all that you **do** want.

Just think about it — you have the opportunity to "get lucky" and allow all the perfect friends, relationships, business opportunities, and money in truck loads to just show up, almost as if you won the lottery (maybe you will!). Luck is on the same vibrational frequency as joy, bliss, passion, appreciation and abundance in all good things.

You can think of your vibrational signal much like a cell

phone frequency that you send out to Source (the Universe). Source always receives and answers your calls, but often- times something goes wrong in the reception at your end. When the signal gets back to you, either you don't hear the call because you can't receive the signal — from either too much noise going on in your head (thinking of things that up- set you), an unclear connection, mixed signal, or too much static — or you have blocked the call altogether because you don't really believe you can have what you want.

In others words, much of the time, we block the call of Source and the desires we are being summoned to. Think back — have you ignored or doubted any moments of inspi- ration you have received? For example a business opportu- nity you turned down, a potential mate you never pursued, or chance to have fun you turned down? When you are inspired and you don't take action on that inspiration, eventually you start to become frustrated because you're not getting any of the good stuff, you have "bad luck," and you feel stuck. This is all because you are not listening and paying attention to any of the good stuff, ideas and thoughts — the inspiration the Universe is presenting you with.

In order to reconnect and receive the calls of inspiration, all you have to do is stop ignoring the calls that are coming to you or sending them to voice mail. Pick up the call and clear the static by beginning to practice thoughts that feel good and your vibrational signal will clear up and get stronger over time. Go towards what you're inspired to try, to do or to be. Follow the yellow brick road. Smell the roses, drink from the well and dare to jump off that cliff into the ocean below. Tell the version of the story that feels good, whether it is true or not, and play, play and then go play some more!

Fun, fun, fun is your only goal and if you see anything that looks and feels remotely fun, do it! Stop looking at your life as it passes you by. Get off the bench. Get up and get into the game and then play your best. Continue to tell your self, "Nothing is more important than feeling good. I will have fun and I will play now!"

Be solid, strong and determined about playing as a way of being. Look for those opportunities that **are** there to play through your life. Play in and with your vibration by making sure the only calls you send out into the universe are ones you want to pick up and receive in return.

Go Play Stop ~ Playing with Your Vibration

Once you get the hang of playing through your life, you may be interested in fun ways you can consciously play around with your personal vibration to see what you can attract. Playing with your vibration is one of the best games you can play with yourself — or you can play with those around you who are interested in conscious creation as well.
Simple Stuff: Start with something you don't have any negative emotion around, like a great parking spot or your favorite food. If it is your favorite dish you want to attract, imagine or pretend you are already eating it. See yourself enjoying it, savoring the flavors. Feel it in your mouth and feel the intensity of the experience as if it is already happening. Now, either let go or continue to enjoy the thought, and allow your Personal Universal Assistant to bring it to you.

Since I started doing this process, my life has become even more fun and is completely shifting in a fantastic direction. One day, I started wanting to attract and own a beautiful, elaborate sports car like a Porche, Tesla or Lamborghini. I physically went and looked at them and took pictures of them. I just thought it would be fun to see if I could simply attract one into my reality.

Within the same day and every day since, I have attracted gorgeous, high-priced cars of various kinds zooming by my path. Whether I am running, watching a movie or driving somewhere, I am attracting lots of fun sports or luxury vehicles without any effort, other than my thoughts. Conscious creation is easy! Now all I do is eagerly anticipate driving and actually owning one. I have confidence my Personal Universal Assistant will bring one into my reality in the perfect timing. **It is very important to not be worried or focused on the time frame in which the Universe will bring it to you.** Be light and easy, allowing the Universe to pick your perfect time.

It Really Works! While in the process of writing this book over the last few months and sending it back and forth between my editor and myself I was eagerly adding the finishing touches on the book I wanted to further share with you how this process or Go Play Stop of Playing With Your Vibration really worked for me. As I continued to play this fun car game and trusting in my Personally Universal Assistant I did physically attract a beautiful brand new car for myself. The car, a 2012 Honda Civic, was not really the sports or luxury car or even the Prius I had been exactly asking for, however, somehow when I went and drove the car, it felt perfect as if this was the one or at least the perfect car for now.

It has an "Eco-Friendly" button that supports the fuel mileage I wanted, getting around 38-42 miles per gallon, looks fun, sleek and sporty and felt good to drive. It was a perfect fit! In addition I was able to get it at the best price with payments I could easily afford. Even the insurance was less than the older vehicle I was driving. The whole time I felt good and the whole process from test drive to purchase completion flowed and felt good. I asked my Universal Personal Assistant for what I wanted and when the inspiration called, I picked up the call, the connection was clear and was acted from and on the inspiration I received.

Master and Get the Big Stuff: Once you have practiced pretending and vibrating the simple stuff into existence, you may be ready for the big stuff. Do you feel confident to take the next step and move onto manifesting bigger and better things, people and experiences into your life? Hopefully, you are believing more and more in your ability to create your life on purpose. If, by chance, you still feel negative emotions around a certain subject, like attracting a playful loving relationship or money, I recommend you continue to build up your "manifesting muscle" and, even better, find ways to play with the negative thought until it feels good or neutral.

Your Power to Go From Fear to Hope

Years ago, I had an opportunity to shift a completely fearful experience into something that I could feel better about. As I have mentioned, I am the mother of five amazing children. When the youngest of the five, Carter, was only nine months old, he became very ill and eventually we had to take him to the hospital. This was the first time Carter had had a hospital experience because, as I described in Chapter 6, he was born at home.

If you recall the beginning of this story from the introduction, Carter had taken ill and my husband and I were growing fearful, as he was starting to turn a blue color. I remember feeling so much pain inside from watching the hospital staff panicking, and from the fear of the unknown of what my baby was experiencing. They whisked him to a children's hospital and we drove ourselves there. My fear increased after the emergency doctor in charge spoke to us, and it became so strong that all I could do was sit down and cry.

The doctors kept telling us that Carter was having trouble breathing on his own, so they had put him on a ventilator and administered a paralytic to keep him breathing. In their attempt to figure out what had gone "wrong" with my son's health, they blamed me for various things — number one, not vaccinating him. After 24 hours, I hadn't slept and my vibration of fear about my son's death was becoming stronger and his health was getting worse.

While talking to one of the doctors about giving him a blood transfusion — they were taking so much blood from him, his sick body could not keep up — I watched as Carter's heart stopped and the team of medical professionals worked to revive him. I could hardly take the physical pain I was experiencing in my body over possibly losing him.

Looking back, I wish I had consciously understood the power of our thoughts and emotions in order to support Carter more. If I had, as hard as it would have been, I think I would have responded differently. At that point in my life, I didn't understand conscious creation, vibration or the Law of Attraction, so I called my friends for help and comfort.

I have two particular friends who were very intuitive and always had a "sense" or feeling about things, so I called to talk to both of them and ask them for guidance. My first friend, Wendy, told me she could feel that Carter hadn't decided whether he was going to continue to stay on the planet or go. She told me she loved me and that as a believer in prayer, she would pray for him and suggested I do the same. My next call was to my close friend, Dixie. Without telling her what Wendy had said, she too felt that he had not made his decision yet. She suggested I help him in the best way possible by telling him I supported whatever he wanted, and so I did.

I went back in the room where he was laying and said, "Carter, I support you in whatever decision you make. I want you to continue to stay with us because I love you. Just relax and allow the doctors to take care of you. I will be here always, I love you!" I felt relief from the fear I had been experiencing and had a sense of peace about the situation. From that point on, I felt a burning desire for Carter's wellness and focused my attention on it.

I had consciously shifted my vibration and was able to feel hopeful about Carter's situation. Within the next 24 hours, Carter began to get better, little by little, until after only 16 days he was released from the hospital. Several doctors escorted Carter out with tears in their eyes — they could not believe he was leaving the hospital alive. They all told me they didn't really believe in miracles, but they had never seen a baby that sick ever leave the hospital perfectly healthy. They never did find out what the "problem" was and it really doesn't matter.

I know beyond a doubt that miracles happen, or are created from our beliefs, thoughts, and feelings. We are all such powerful creators; we really do have the power to shift our vibration, and even influence the vibrations of others, in a direction that can and will change circumstances and events to our advantage. My husband believes that my hopefulness and focus on Carter's wellness was the miracle in his recovery, and now that I know about and believe in the Law of Attraction and vibrational alignment, I do too.

Life can be so fun, magical and playful if only you will see and feel it as so. What may seem hard to do is actually simple. To get what you want, simply focus on thoughts that cause you to feel good. When you encounter a situation that does not feel good, find a way to shift it by focusing on the situation as a gift and what it has caused you to want. I had never wanted one of my children to be more well and healthy than when Carter was sick, and you may never want money more than when you feel that you don't have any. You have the power to see every situation as another opportunity to gain clarity in your life.

You don't have to understand why you are experiencing something in your life that doesn't look or feel good, however, if you want it to turn around and go in a positive direction, let go, surrender or give it to your Personal Universal Assistant to take care of. Go do something fun, go on vacation or imagine the best possible outcome. Say to yourself, "I don't know why this is happening, but I do know somehow it always works out." The Universe will take care of you and bring you all good things if you allow it to.

Go Play Stop ~ Pretending and Imagining

Here is a playful game you can play upon waking in the morning, going to bed at night or anytime you have a moment to yourself. It uses your imagination and gets you pretending — I feel so childlike when I think about pretending! Pretending is much like *intending,* except you envision more vivid images and scenarios to support your intention/vision, and this aligns your energy with your point of attraction.

Think back to when you were young and you would play pretend. I remember putting on my mom's long-haired, blonde wig and purple dress. In my imagination, the wig became my flowing blonde hair and the bright purple dress was a beautiful flowing, sparkling gown with diamond buttons. I completed this ensemble with a pair of my mom's high heels and a few pieces of jewelry. In my imagination, I was a gorgeous and glamorous movie star and I felt like it too. My mom took pictures of me and I imagined she was an important photographer wanting my picture and autograph.

Looking back on those pictures of me in that outfit, I look nothing like the image I still hold in my head, but I don't really care about the "reality" of those images because the memories are so grand. At that time in my life, I always had what I needed and wanted. My parents treated me special during those times and I felt special too. My whole life felt magical and it wasn't even "real!"

A few years later, when I stopped pretending about my glamorous, movie star life (or rarely anything else for that matter), my life took a different turn. Instead of pretending, I gave my attention to what was going wrong in my life. I felt out of the flow and eventually I was completely unhappy and blamed others constantly for what I was attracting. Like many people, I just didn't know better.

Years and years later, only after really understanding the Law of Attraction — my vibration and the fact that I was creating my own reality with my thoughts and emotions — did I start to take full responsibility for my life, and start pretending again. Just the other day, I was pretending that I received a large check in the mail, and that same day I got a letter in the mail saying my mom had left me $25,000.

A friend of mine was engaged and wanted to simply receive a diamond for his wife to be. He sat down and imagined the whole idea of the diamond and what it would feel like presenting it to her. The next day while sitting in an airport waiting for his plane, he picked up a magazine that was lying on the seat next to him. He was very early and was one of the only people sitting there. When he opened the magazine, a princess-cut yellow diamond fell out and onto his lap!

Wait, there's more! He had the diamond mounted and officially presented it to his love. When she saw the diamond, she was overjoyed and couldn't believe her eyes. She told her love that years ago she had imagined a princess-cut, yellow diamond as her wedding ring, but had forgotten about it altogether until she saw the ring he so lovingly gave her. The Universe worked (or played) its magic to bring these two people together with the perfect diamond in the most perfect timing.

This Law of Attraction and vibration alignment stuff is fun and powerful. Just watch how amazing your life becomes when you constantly and consistently adopt a fun, loving, playful attitude. Imagine and pretend that your life is completely fun and playful all the time, and it will be. Just pretend the possibilities of whatever you want and record the synchronicities that start to "magically" happen. Even though you will feel as if the vibrational matching stuff is magical, it is not magic — it is for real. You create your own magic, luck, and life, simply and easily, by the thoughts and emotions you choose to focus upon.

For fun and play, if you are not currently in a playful loving relationship, have a pretend conversation in the car with your imaginary soon-to-be-arriving mate. Imagine what he/she looks like, things he/she says, and the way you feel by being with him/her. Imagine how you feel being a part of the most wonderful relationship and conversation — laughing and having the best time ever. The more you can feel good and pretend/imagine this person as if they already exist, the faster he/she will show up — and be even more amazing than you envisioned.

The Universe loves to give you everything you want, and in even better form/timing/ways than you can ever imagine. Believing, knowing and trusting that the Universe is on your side can be such a relief and comfort. Yes, the Universe will also give you what you don't want, if you focus on that, but it really likes to give you want you do want, so just start pretending what you want and know it is already yours. Playfully vibrate your life into being the way you want it to be. Again, remember every day, in every way there is always an opportunity to play, so you can vibrate/create even more playful possibilities.

12

TELL A NEW FUN STORY

Why Play!
It's time to shred the unhappy stories and
Play to create your new story
full of fun and adventure!

Things That Make Us Smart

Stories have the felicitous capacity of capturing exactly those elements that formal decision methods leave out. Logic tries to generalize, to strip the decision making from the specific context, capture the emotions.... Stories are important cognitive events, for they encapsulate, into one compact package, information, knowledge, context and emotion.

Don Norman

Have you found yourself feeling lost, scared, or like you'll never know/achieve your purpose, dreams and desires? This usually occurs when we either focus on the stories of our past, our future, or the stories we tell ourselves that can't have something, we are not good enough or worthy enough to receive. In order to free yourself of the old stories that you tell about why you don't have what you want, you must create a new story full of all the possibilities that lay in front of you. Within the old story is the bright new story, just waiting to be told. Then, your only job is to let the new story in and allow the Universe to make it come true.

We have all experienced emotional hurt and pain. The pain is experienced because of the thoughts we think and the story we tell about our interpretation of the situation. *Story... sharpens our understanding of one thing by showing it in the context of something else.* (Daniel Pink *A Whole New Mind*) The stories in our minds are simply our understanding of the context we have created in our mind. If you want to change or alter the story of your life, you have to consciously re-create a new story, replace the old story and start telling the new story, perhaps even replaying it consistently in your mind until it sticks. Attachment to the old story will continue to bring you pain — release it and find a better, more playful story to tell and you will begin to feel differently from the inside out.

Letting in the New Story

People often wonder why is it so hard to let go of the attachment to the old story. Take the example of the breakup of a relationship. It's difficult because you are attached to an idea or belief, and not really the person. A person is a reflection of yourself in some form, and when you have expanded in a new direction, the old reflection no longer fits and you feel out of alignment. But it's often the *idea* of being in a relationship that's hard to detach from.

Another analogy would be when someone loses a large amount of body fat. They might have enjoyed the clothes they once wore but the old clothes no longer fit. It is time for a new wardrobe or to create new clothes from the old.

Let's look at relationships again. Suppose you met someone new and felt an immediate connection like it was a complete match, perhaps because they wanted someone who needed them and you felt needy — like the old clothes, you both fit perfectly. Over time, you grew, changed and expanded, and then you no longer felt needy and instead enjoyed being and feeling more free. The new relationship story you begin to tell includes two people who both feel secure within themselves and the objective would be to enjoy one another's company, without any neediness.

Does this mean that the original person you gave your

affection to can't become a newly expanded version as well? Of course they can, and through your easy-going, pure thoughts of appreciation and love for them, they may become a match after all. Your partner, through your new attention and focus on their positive aspects, will either become your new perfect match or they will easily flow out and a new person will flow in. Either way, that is not your job but the job of the Universe.

However, if you hold on to an idea, person or story from the perspective of lack — such as "this is the only person in the world who could possibly love me" — you will push them farther away rather than bring them (or the idea) closer to you. The key is to consistently see this person, idea or story in a newly expanded, abundant light, as if it already exists, and let go of the old version altogether. If you take a moment to write down and read the old story, you may realize that the old version was no longer working for you anyway; then letting in the new becomes easier.

Go Play Stop ~ Creating Your New Stories

Step 1: Decide what new supportive story you will tell. You will know what new story to tell from the details of the old. For example, my old story of my mom was that she did not like me and thought I was a difficult child. This old story made me feel bad every time I told it. So, I made a conscious decision to no longer tell this relationship story of my mom and me, and instead I made up a new one. After all, maybe my perception of my childhood was wrong — how can I really know what my mother's thoughts were? I have no true way of knowing, seeing or experiencing the world from her point of view.

So, I tell it like I want it to be: *my mother and I loved one another and like her, I am a very out-going and playful person. I love the example my mom was to me, always playing around, joking and laughing. She loved to talk and so do I. She sang beautifully. I learned so much from her example of how to support and serve others and have fun in life.* This new story has many true elements I had not focused on before, that is, until I started to look for the new story within the old story of the past.

In making up a new story, you can tell it any way you want it to be — it doesn't necessarily need to be true, "real" or factual, as long as you feel good telling it.

Step 2: Once you have created your new story, tell it as often as possible. Imagine the story from the perspective that it is already happening or did happen just the way you tell it. In time, you will start to see the evidence of your new story becoming real. When I started telling my new story about my childhood, my relationship with my mother "magically" improved and our feelings towards one another were all of a sudden completely loving. "When you change the way you look at things, the things you look at change" (Dr. Wayne Dyer).

Step 3: Continue to visualize the new story so completely that you convince yourself that it is real. That is why playing around with your imagination and pretending is a very important part of the game. When you pretend or play through a subject it becomes real. As long as you continue to pretend and play around with your new story, you will begin to feel good. Feeling good brings more situations and experiences that feel good until every story in your life will eventually have happy endings, new beginnings and lots of fun in between.

You may be thinking "but it isn't *true.* I am just fooling myself." We are always fooling ourselves — you might as well create a happy story instead of an equally inaccurate unhappy one with you starring as the main victim. There is always a sunny side to any truth; look for that and ignore, or don't give any energy to, any other side. And then fool yourself so thoroughly you don't even remember the old story you used to tell.

Creating Your Life

No matter what, continue to tell your new story the way you want it to be because the new story you create, begin to tell, and think about will, over time, become your new reality. I love the way Seth (Jane Roberts) talks about the reality we create:

> You create your reality according to your beliefs and expectations; therefore, it behooves you to examine them carefully.
>
> If you do not like your world, then examine your own expectations. Every thought in one way or another is constructed by you in physical terms. Your world is formed in faithful replica of your own thoughts....
>
> [Tell yourself] I am an individual. I form my physical environment. I change and make my world. I am free of time and space. I am a part of all that is. There is no place within me that creativity does not exist. (from *The Seth Material*).

This is a powerful message for creating the life experience you want to have. Spend time writing down your thoughts, beliefs and the stories you have been telling. But be careful — every time you recall stories of the past that cause you to feel negative emotions, you risk recreating circumstances and experiences that will match this past feeling. Do not get wound up in thoughts of the past; make a new story. In the face of adversity, you must be able to maintain the thoughts and feeling of what you do want or you will end up stressed out and then creating more of what you do **not** want.

Think about what your true purpose is as a powerfully-focused, conscious creator. You came to this time/space reality to expand through contrast and then to practice aligning with all your true desires. There is really nothing you need to do, learn or know except to continue to stay focused on feeling good, playing and having fun. Let go of any thoughts and stories of your life that are not in alignment with what you really want and what you want to create. You are the story teller, creator and lover of your life experience and you are the only one who has the power to change it.

By your attention to thoughts that feel good, eventually instant manifestation will be yours. Remind yourself constantly: "I am the creator of my own life experience. Everything I think, feel and speak of is a creation-in-progress as I vibrate it to be." Create stories of love, your dreams fulfilled and the abundance you already have. To give your stories power, focus your thoughts, words and emotions into them. When thoughts, emotions or experiences come forth that do not feel good, stop and think to yourself *how can I turn this situation into a better, even playful, story?*

You are Already There

Many people have theorized that time is only an illusion and that the past, present and future are happening at the same time. If this is true, then you are already there, here and expanded to your new form and in your new story. Iyanla Vanzant, writer and spiritual teacher, put it so eloquently when she wrote:

> You are the love you seek. You are the companionship you desire. You are your own completion, your own wholeness. You are your best friend, your confidant. 'You are,' as poetess Audre Lourde wrote, 'the one that you are looking for.' You are the only one who can do what you are looking for someone else to do (from *In the Meantime: Finding Yourself and the Love You Want*).

The times in my life when I have been most unhappy, I was caught up in focusing on my weaknesses instead of my strengths, noticing my flaws instead of my beauty, or running from my fears instead of facing them with love. I thought I had to be everything to everyone and the best at everything. My job was to be the perfect mother, wife, housekeeper, you name it. I had to be perfect and in control of everything and everyone. I was consistently focused on what I wasn't doing right, his was a battle with myself that I was losing myself in and to. Everyone around me could feel my raging vibration of pain and anger, and all I wanted to do was escape from me and my life.

One day, the cracks in my life I had created became big holes and I fell through. I became someone I no longer liked because I was no longer fun; I had stopped playing. I felt lost and alone. Within one year of "no fun", I manifested a life full of pain and within one month— my husband of 14 years said he no longer felt "connected and in love" with me and instead had started to develop affectionate feelings towards another woman. Two weeks later after I heard this news, My 20-year-old son became addicted to drugs, committed a major crime and was sentenced to prison for a minimum of 37 months. A week or so later, my oldest daughter also started using drugs and chose to give up custody of her two small children because of her addiction, and the next day, my 16-year-old daughter moved in with her dad, saying she no longer wanted to live with me and rarely wanted to see me. Lastly, within 6 months, my mother died and we found out my mom had spent all of the money my dad had left her and mortgaged the her house to the maximum trying to take care of my sister and her two kids, leaving no money to bury her.

Wow, what a story I can tell, right? I am telling you my old story to illustrate a point about storytelling. Yes, you could say it is all true; these situations and events did happen and I did have a part in co-creating them; however, it is still just one version of the whole story. The facts, events and experiences are always only a part of a story. That old story leaves out so much — all the amazing things that happened. When a flower grows up in the cracks in the cement, each one of us has the choice of what to see: the cracks or the beauty of the flower.

The fun and playful story I want to tell is how my life, over that same year, despite all the tragedy, was actually amazing. At the start of the year, I had some incredible, life-changing moments. I learned about the rules of money, started saving money and, at the same time, paying off debts for the first time in my adult life. I lost 25 pounds and looked the best I ever have at 40 years of age. I was inspired again to play and changed my life around! At the end of that "year from hell" (which wasn't really), I wrote this book and started a Play Movement.

More than ever, I learned so much about conscious creation and the law of attraction that I have continued to increase my income every month since. My two youngest children and I spend more time playing together. I feel happier and more fulfilled as a mother than ever before. These two young men, Mitchel and Carter, are doing amazing in home school and they even enjoy making me yummy food now.

For the first time in my life, I have one of the best girlfriend's who has almost the exact same interests, future expectations and beliefs. She is so fun! She feels like a friend I would have had (but didn't) when I was 14. We both feel so young and frisky when we start talking about boys (men), the Law of Attraction, and of course, I play with her on the phone or through text messages.

The most important part of that fateful year came at the moment I realized my passion/purpose and what I could do to inspire others. From the time I was little, I had a burning desire to find a way to run my own business or do something purposeful to inspire others — something that would be life-giving to me and to them. Playing lights me up and giving others permission and inspiration on how to play feels even better than I imagined.

This new story, or the feeling-good part of my story, is full of high-vibrational excitement, joy and inspiration all in one. You too can choose which story to tell and what to see from your vantage point that feels good to you. Feel free to add color to your story by making yourself extra-awesome — as the person you want to become, as if you are already there and already know everything you need to know... because in the illusion of the future, you are already there.

Go Play Stop ~ Make Up Stories

My mom used to make up stories the way she wanted them to be rather than the way they were. Her versions were always the best — the most elaborate stories compared to our versions of the truth. My younger sister couldn't stand that my mom did this and would embarrass her all the time by calling her out in front of others over the truth. My mom was right — it wasn't lying — it was simply her attempt to feel good and make her life the way she wanted it to be. She made feeling good more important than the "truth."

I miss my mom's story telling. It doesn't matter if the stories she told of me as a baby were true or not because it just feels good remembering. Would it really matter if when you met a new person you told them your fanciful version of your story? Perhaps you could make yourself out to be a millionaire, an actor who just received a major role you aren't allowed to discuss, a ridiculously successful entrepreneur, or perhaps you could say you are happily married, even if don't really feel you are.

It's no wonder we stop pretending when all around us we are told (or we tell ourselves) to be truthful all the time. The problem is if our story doesn't feel good, then we just recreate the same vibrational experience over and over again. We often lie to protect others from being hurt or from being angry with us, yet we are brutally honest with ourselves, which usually isn't very helpful. A harmless, fun, and playful story about a life you wish you had is great because the more you tell these stories about your dreams with feel-good emotions, the more they will come true. Go ahead and tell a fictional story, and it will become true, because the Law of Attraction will make it *real.*

When you're feeling down, go for a ride, meet a new friend and tell a fun, playful story. This may inspire them and it will cause you to feel much better. One of the best things about this life experience is that we all have the chance to make up/create the life we wish to live. Remind yourself that in every day and in every way, there is always an opportunity to tell a playful story so you can feel good now!

13

Dress In Your Play Attitude

Why Play!
In the morning, put on your play attitude
and you will have the best day ever!

Teal's Ten Tidbits for Today

Smile with your whole body. Raise your arms over your head and wiggle your fingers to create a smile. It will get your heart beating faster which is always good. (1 minute)

Hug yourself. Wrap your arms around yourself and give yourself a big squeeze. Feel the love that you exude from your arms. (1 minute)

Dance. Turn up the music and move! Get those body parts moving! As little as two minutes will get your heart beating and improve your heart health. (2 minutes)

Look strangers that you pass in the eye, give them a wink, and a big smile! Some will smile back, some won't but they will all remember that someone tried to make their day a little brighter! (Six people equals 1 minute)

Wear your favorite color. It can be in a piece of jewelry or necktie. Heck, it can even be your undies! The pleasure you feel from having your color with you will brighten your outlook. (No time, you have to get dressed anyway!)

Read a favorite book or magazine for at least 10 minutes. This will give your brain a break from all the information we must process during the day. Reading something of your choice refreshes your brain thus allowing you to accomplish more during your day. (10 minutes)

Surround yourself with favorite scents. It can be as simple as wearing a favorite fragrance or aftershave, spray a pleasant room spray, or keep a fragrant candle nearby. If you can't burn the candle, get one that is not in a jar. Rub it between your hands several times a day and the scent will fill your immediate space. (1 minute) (I recommend www.everydayeclectic.com)

Walk outside for 5 minutes. This gets your heart pumping and the vitamin D generates serotonin, the "feel good" chemical, in your brain. Even if it is cloudy or rainy, the sun is still creating light so it is beneficial. (5 minutes)

Write 3 things in a journal every day that creates a feeling of appreciation in you. This allows you to focus on the positive you are a part of every day. (5 minutes)

Put yourself first for 21 minutes every day. That leaves you 23 hours and 39 minutes to focus on the rest of the world. When you are happier, the world around you will follow your lead of happiness!

These tips have inspired me to always stay young, feel good and have fun each and every day!

Joyce A. Teal

Each morning when you wake, get up and get ready for the day. Before you walk out the door or get busy doing the stuff on your to-do list, it is most important that you slip into your *play attitude.* Why, you ask? Because play looks and feels good on you. You shine in play and you are the sexiest, most confident person when you put on your fun and playful self.

What is a Play Attitude?

We are often encouraged to dress for success, as if the

clothes you wear will all of a sudden magically change you into a success. But is it really the suit that makes the man, or the man that makes the suit look good? I know we all understand that if we want to go out on a date to a fancy restaurant or get a high paying job, we need to look our best, but beyond clothes, it's our attitude that really creates our day and sets our life in motion. In Daniel Pink's book "A Whole New Mind" he discusses research that has been done on one of the indicators of a person's success is her/his personality. Thank goodness it's not the brain, I was worried about that one, afraid I wouldn't have a chance at success myself... hehehaha

One morning I woke up and made the best decision for myself... I would wake up each day and find as many ways to play as possible. I'd never felt so happy or playful in my adult life before. The only "bad" thing was, at the time, I didn't understand how to make it last, that is until I did the play experiment again and realized it all started with my beliefs and attitude first. You see, the way you continue to view the world and respond to others has a lot to do with your attitude.

Your attitude comes from the thoughts and beliefs you have about yourself. If you are unsure about yourself, your attitude is generally timid and shy, and your body language is closed and inward. On the other hand, if you love and adore yourself, you stand tall, confident and your attitude is generally open and welcoming. The really cool thing about attitudes and beliefs is they can always change.

A belief is nothing more than a thought you have practiced thinking and feeling. So, you can always change your beliefs and in turn, change your attitude. You can also change your belief and your attitude by pretending. I know, you may wonder why I keep bringing up the subject of **playfully pretending**, but you would be amazed just how much your life can change when you pretend and can believe what you pretend to be true or at least a very big possibility. Not only that, you will have so much fun doing it.

Deciding on your attitude is no harder than putting on your clothes. It's easy to put on a playful attitude and when you do, you will feel and look like a million bucks — or at least like someone who is fun to be with! A play attitude is much like a confident attitude, except more inviting and youthful. A play attitude includes a smile so big your cheeks may begin to hurt. You laugh easily, your eyes sparkle with excitement, and you make eye contact with everyone you greet. Your playful spirit *shines*!

Your personality glows and your heart is open to all. You believe that a stranger is only a friend you haven't met yet and you are always ready to meet new friends. Your life is full and fun, and you attract playful opportunities everywhere you go. With your play attitude on, you may not be liked by everyone (overtly happy people are not always favored/tolerated by the unhappy) but you will always be remembered.

How to Dress the Playful Part

A play attitude is so fun to wear that when you practice it, pretend it, and do it enough, you will feel and look lighter, brighter and always ready to play. The first key to putting on your play attitude is to make a decision that you want to experience a more playful life. Decisions, decisions, decisions....

Every decision you make, consciously or unconsciously, alters the course of your life. Even when you are not making any decisions, or when you don't know what to do, you are still doing *something,* still making a decision. You will go out into the world with some sort of attitude — why not make your attitude one of fun and joy? You have everything to gain and nothing to lose.

Once you decide that you want to experience more of the playful side of life and you're ready to slip into your own personal always-perfecting fitting play attitude, make sure to put on clothing that will match this attitude as well. If you wear a suit and tie, wear a fun tie that will let others know you mean fun. It is always important to wear the outfits that cause you to feel fun and playful. I find that as a playful woman, light, airy (even fairy, as I like to imagine I am a magical Play Fairy) dresses match my play attitude perfectly. If you have to wear a uniform, do your best to do something as fun as you can get away with — buttons, a hat, or even fun underwear and tee shirts.

In reality, it is not the clothes you wear but the *attitude* you wear that counts. Now that you are ready to head out, do a "mirror check" and make sure your play attitude is shining through. Think about how you will playfully approach people and set the intention that you are open to any playful opportunities that come your way.

Go Play Stop ~ What to Do With a Play Attitude

I find that there is not much you need to do when you're dressed to the hilt in your play attitude — except play. If your smile is as big as it can be and you are paying (playing) attention to others, looking them straight in the eyes, that alone will send the message that you are approachable and kind. People are naturally drawn to those who stand tall and look confident and fun.

When you're standing in line at a store, make it a point to talk to others and make a new friend every day. Offer to let another person go ahead of you, and ask them about their day. If they have a child, that is the best way to start to play because kids are experts. I have noticed that kids can spot a player from miles away. They will know if you are the real deal, and they sure enjoy an adult who knows how to play.

Instead of just walking into a building or to your car, skip or dance. Instead of quietly standing in the elevator, whistle or sing. If you are eating alone at work or in a restaurant, invite another person who is alone to join you. If you have a roller coaster close enough, use your lunch break or after-work time to ride it. Take a cab and offer someone waiting for a cab to join you — tell them the ride is on you.

Buy a homeless person a meal, and then sit and ask him about his life. You never know what stories you will hear. On a free day, stand out with a sign offering free hugs. It is amazing how energizing hugs can be for you and the person you're hugging. Go to a retirement center and take a note book or game; then sit with a person who looks like they need a friend and play a game with them or ask them to tell you their life story.

Take a walk in nature, talk to the animals, and be in the moment appreciating the beauty that surrounds you. Volunteer at a hospital to hold babies or play with children who are sick — you could even dress up in something fun and tell jokes to bring laughter to their day. Talk to your neighbor, or invite a friend or new coworker to lunch and offer to pay.

There are so many possibilities that will come to mind when you are wearing your play attitude. A play attitude is inspiring, inviting and gives others you encounter permission to be playful, too. All great leaders lead by example and create leaders. Be who you are. Know who you really are, because you are a part of this life experience to have fun and be unique.

You Are Perfect

You are one of a kind and there is no one like you. Your play attitude is unique; it will be different than mine or another's. Your play attitude doesn't have to be pure giddiness, if that doesn't suit your personality, but it will be child-like, whatever that looks like for you. The key to a true play attitude is that your thoughts, feelings and desires revolve around playing and having the best time ever. You already know how to play — it is within you because you were born knowing that your primary intent on this planet was to have as much fun as humanly possible.

With a playful attitude and your focus on play, in no time at all you will be playing through your life in every way. Feeling good and having fun is the only thing you need to focus on in order to get all the abundance, relationships and stuff you want; when you do so, you are in vibrational alignment for all good things to come.

Giving, allowing and playing with others offer you the chance to connect and remind others how amazing we all are. At some point in the past, we diverged from our tribal communities and yet no matter what we do, each one of us still craves the fun and playfulness found within true human connection.

You don't need to like another to flirt — it's just a playful connection. You don't need to know how to dance or sing, just do it. The only judgment is the one we place upon ourselves. Acceptance attracts acceptance, love attracts love, and play attracts play. You don't have to know anything other than who you really are.

Dale Carnegie taught that if you want to make a true human connection, you must first give others what they need first. Maybe all you have to offer is a smile and kind thought but that, my friend, is **priceless** — everybody wants to know that they are cared about and important. I will be the first to say, now and forever, that I genuinely love you and appreciate you just for being you.

You and I live in a world with billions of others, and even if we are the only ones playing and giving out smiles, kind words and encouraging others to join us, eventually there will be many people doing it. Face Book and other social networks are so popular because we all desire connection with others. The internet is one of the most fantastic inventions of our time in its ability to provide a space for information exchange and connection... but it cannot and will never replace the love and attention you can give to another face to face and heart to heart.

Take five minutes to dress in your play attitude every day, and then go out there in the world and share it will others. You matter, you are important and you are everything you need to be now. You affect the lives of others and you have the opportunity to affect even more, simply by being loving, kind and playful always. Today and every day, slip into your play attitude and love yourself, your family, your friends, your community and the world — they will all love you back more!

14

YOUR LIFE CAN BE A PARTY EVERYDAY!

Why Play!
Get out of your head,
into your heart
and lead with your playful spirit...
that's when magic happens!

Here you are, at the last chapter of *Play Is The New Way!*
And, hopefully, by now, you have already begun to play. I
have given you an understanding of play and how important
it is to your well-being, health and happiness. You are
loaded with play ideas to inspire your playful spirit to come
out and join you, and today, you are dressed in your play attitude, excited to make play a part of your every day, right?

Play happens naturally when we lead with our hearts instead of our heads. If you allow play to be a part of the flow
of your life, in no time, your life will become a playful party
every day. Except for birthdays, I find holidays like Christmas
and Valentine's to be less than desirable. We don't need a
holiday to remind us to give appreciation, love, gifts, and to
have fun — we can choose to make every day a celebration,
because it *is!*

You are on an extended vacation in your human form,
and I can't say this enough because I really want it to seep
into every crevice of your body, mind, and ego. Your
soul/inner being already knows and has been trying to get
the message through since you were young. Are you really
ready? All senses open and available? Here it is: **life is
supposed to be fun and playful!**

Your real joy is in playing, and the only thing you need to do is to have fun and enjoy the contrast, both positive and negative, along the way. Let in all your desires by having fun and feeling good by playing! Make every day a "walking on sunshine" kind of day!

When you put on your play attitude, you will waltz out into the world, ready and available to make each day more special, more amazing and more fun than the day before. The good stuff and people will start to magically appear in your life and joy, freedom and exhilaration will constantly be yours. You won't have to search for Mr. or Ms. Right — they will show up and they will be playful, too.

Follow your gut — the tingles and the pulls in your heart. They will lead you down the path of least resistance. How many times have you read about those that are already rich, happy and successful in every way possible, and you wanted to know, "Why not me?" It's because they know the secret of playing through life, being happy and joyous, and making sure they feel good all the time.

Invite Everything and Everyone to Your Playful Party

You have every possibility, opportunity, secret, and solution to be "blissed-out" now. Joseph Campbell advised us all to "follow your bliss!" Bliss is the stuff dreams are created with, and when you combine your dreams, your burning desires and feeling good now, you have the recipe for a playful party. Isn't it time to feel good now? Feel good enough of the time and all the doors will open and the best people, most fun adventures and endless amounts of money will simply and easily flow in without any *hard* work and least of all *stress.*

Your beautifully packaged, gold-sealed, personalized invitations are presented to everyone and everything by your high-vibrating, amazingly positive, joyful feelings. You don't even create the invitations — your Personal Universal Assistant does it for you, because you are the star of the whole party. People show up for you, the stuff you've asked for is given to you, and you just get to dance around and have fun.

Affect Others

Isn't it powerful to know that you get to be, do, and have everything you want, and that your life is your creation? Of course, you may not like the sound of that right now, because maybe your life isn't what you would like it to be, but you have all the power you need to change it and make it into your perfect life. Take the "bad times" in your life as an example or just an experience of what you do not want, then you can move forward, learning and growing from the experience by focusing on what the difficult experience caused you to want instead. This process will allow your life to become so grand that you will inspire and influence others to create their own fun and playful party regardless of their difficult times.

My daughter Danyell, who was for a time in her life was experiencing such pain over the thoughts she would think and then feel about herself began taking drugs, like heroine, as a means to escape from herself and those negative thoughts. Today she understands and knows that the only escape from those negative self destructive thoughts is to replace them with thoughts that do feel better. After only a few months of self love and forgiveness she has completely shifted her life in a whole new direction. Danyell, 23 years, is currently writing a book to support and inspire other teenagers and young adults to understand how to love and appreciate themselves using their power to support themselves and not to self destruct.

You not only affect your own life, you affect the lives of others. Of course, you are not *responsible* for the lives and creations of others, but you do have the ability, through the vibration of your thoughts and feelings, to influence others. Danyell tells me everyday how much of an influence I am in her life because I don't tell her how to be or what to do, I am simply an example and an inspiration to and for her. There is

no need to get others to follow you in your fun and play —
there is only inspiration. Inspiration to influence others
comes naturally from your connection to who you really are.

Who you really are is a physically-focused spiritual being, born of a playful spirit. You were born a player and you
will come back to play again. If you forgot how to play and
enjoy your life experience, it is because you started leading
your life from your mind/ego and focusing on what's wrong in
your life and not what's right. When you make play a part of
your life again, you will create a better, more playful life, you
will remind others what's most important, and you will show
them the way by your example.

Go Play Stop ~ More Ways to Make Your Life a Playful Party Every Day

Down to Up: When you're feeling down and you
want to turn your frown upside down, turn on your favorite
music and dance. If you're in the groove of a bad mood,
head out for a run, a walk, a hike, and listen to someone that
will help you turn your groove into a good mood. When you
receive some bad news, like you lost your job, remind yourself that perhaps this is simply the Universe's way of sending
you a new, better job or business opportunity.

You have four good options when you're feeling down:
think better feeling thoughts, distract yourself with thoughts
that feel good, find a way to play, or give in. Giving in is
when you let go and let the Universe take the wheel. Getting
to a place where you deeply know that all is perfect and you
just can't see the next step is part of completely trusting in
All-that-is.

I love how Kevin Trudeau talks about your radar
screens. The radar screen is like a small TV screen, and you
are only able to see a small portion of what the Universe has
in store for you. For example, if you have been vibrationally
asking for a better relationship, and then one day your mate
asks you for a divorce, that is only seeing a small section of
the whole picture. You may want to perceive this situation as

a bad thing until a year later when you meet a new mate who is a perfect match to the better relationship you always wanted.

Every "bad" situation can have a golden outcome if only you can remain focused on feeling good, no matter what. Through your "bad" experiences, ask for changes, and the Universe answers, but sometimes in order for the Universe to give you something better, it clears away the old. Yes, somehow you were a match to the negative situation that occurred in your life. Now, instead of focusing on what happened, turn your attention to the positive aspects of your life, and everything will go so much smoother and all the good stuff will come your way quickly.

That is why the practice of creating a playful party in life is so important. Take the negative situations in your life lightly and with an optimistic perspective. Imagine you were playing a video game and your turn ended because you lost, and all you have to do is restart the game and play again. You have a chance to play again each time you wake in the morning — for that matter, each and every moment throughout your day. Your positive vibrational thoughts and feelings are always more powerful than the negative ones.

Now that you know your vibrations create your reality, you might worry about what you have been emitting lately — don't. Just start now, playing and feeling good again. The more you practice playing and feeling good, the harder it will become to feel bad. When you start to feel bad, it will feel so uncomfortable after feeling so good that you won't stay there very long any more.

Dream and Appreciate: When you are feeling high on life, or even just neutral, that's the time to go play by trying on your new desires. Go sit in or test drive your future car. If you love jewelry, visit your favorite jeweler and put on diamonds. Looking for a new place to live? Find a few open houses with something close to your dream home and take the tour. Find pictures of your favorite stuff on the internet and make a movie out of it all and watch it every day, or print out the pictures and put them up all over the place.

Create a dream board or book and write down all your dreams as you are inspired. When you feel especially good, keep it going by appreciating every person and aspect of your life as it is now. Often times we think that if we appreciate what we already have that it will prevent us from attracting more of what we really want, that we will instead continue to attract more of what we already have. But, the opposite is true, the more you appreciate what you already have the more you will attract the experiences, people, money and things that match that vibration.

Similar to the way a dollar bill can multiply into a million over the course of a month, your thought and focus of appreciation over your current life experience can multiply into a life that looks, feels and is million times better than before. Purchase or design a beautiful separate note book specifically created for your appreciating thoughts. The more you appreciate what you already have, the more you will have and the better you will feel when you do.

Feed Your Playful Spirit: You can keep your playful party going through the thoughts you think, the time you spend clearing your mind, and feeding yourself the best nutrition.

I find that listening to/watching positive, uplifting people and movies keeps me in alignment with feeling good. For years, I have listened to successful people, from Dr. Wayne Dyer to Mark Victor Hansen to Abraham-Hicks and Louise Hay. Each of these individuals recommends listening to them and other successful people in order to keep your mind fresh and focused. No matter what you want to be successful at, listen to or read those that know their stuff and have done something similar to what you want to do accomplish.

Just as feeding your body whole, organic fresh foods is important, so too is feeding your mind with information and inspiration that feels good when you see it and/or hear it. Luckily, we are all a part of the digital age of technology. My iPhone can do so many things, including hold books, audio books, music and more. When I go running or when I am driving, I listen to inspiring, successful individuals and this keeps me positively focused and feeds my spirit.

It is easier to change your life when you have someone you feel inspired to mirror. Just imagine how many women and men are constantly inspired from people like Oprah, Lance Armstrong or Michael Jordan? These individuals can mentor you from their inspiring lives and accomplishments just by studying them. They are people just like you, they breathe in and out, they eat food and they bleed when they're hurt.

What I am trying to say is *they are just as special as you are* — the only "magic" they have is a strong belief in their self, a burning desire to achieve their dream and an ability to feel good most of the time. They have allowed themselves to be a vibrational match to what they wanted by staying focused on the positive aspects of their lives. Listening to them, studying them, and playing through your life to feel good will yield you the same or even better results.

Oh, the Places You'll Go!

All good things come to an end to allow for new, fabulous beginnings. I hope your days are happier, your nights shine brighter and your whole life feels more wonderful than ever. You now have back in your tool box the tool that fixes everything, the one-size-fits-all and looks perfect on all outfits, the time tested, totally proven, 100% solution to every problem, situation or experience... **PLAY**!

> You have brains in your head. You have feet in your shoes. You can steer yourself any direction you choose. You're on your own. And you know what you know. And YOU are the one who'll decide where to go... (Dr. Seuss, *Oh, the Places You'll Go!*)

Yes, it's up to you now; actually, it has always been within your power to direct and decide where you will go in your life, what you will do and how you will get there. Your imagination and playful spirit will make your journey in life more fun, brighter and more colorful. I am so excited for you, that you've learned to play in the only way that uniquely you can.

Your path is bright, my friend. The doors are open and the sails are full. The lights are on you because you are the **STAR**. There is no more "book of excuses," for you have thrown out that book and now you have the best book of all — the how-to-play book and it's there for all. Dr. Seuss has always been my hero; he understood that "being crazy isn't enough," that you also need to use your imagination, live for your dreams and wake up looking through a new lens on life and see it in the most enjoyable way.

Play is the New Way was written from inspiration to offer you a new playful telescope through which to see the world — fresh, new and fun. Your playful party is waiting — there's no limit or time and all are invited to join. All you have to do is put on your play attitude and go play. Your horse and carriage, or Rolls Royce, will take you anywhere you want to go because I promise you 100% — dreams really do come true! **Play is the new way,** and every day, in every way, there is *always* an opportunity to have fun and play!

For more fun and inspiration on how to play, visit www.GoPlazy.com and come play at one of the fun Play Shoppes.

Oh the plays you will play, when you *Go Play!*

AFTERWORD

There are times in our lives when we decide that "good enough" is no longer enough and we may even begin to ask ourselves questions like, "Is this all there is in life?" This restlessness is good as it generally causes a conscious shift or an awakening and reconnection to your spiritual self. Of course, you instinctively know there is more to and in life. . .a lot more, and you have the opportunity to have, do and be more! And you deserve to have it all!

The purpose of this simple little play book is to easily and simply inspire an awakening and understanding for you to live your life to the fullest, have FUN and PLAY along the way! You have the right to claim what you really want and desire! You deserve not to "work hard" but instead to Play More! This is not to say you may not spend hours a day on a project, book or job. You probably will. The difference can be that you will have fun and feel good or even great while doing it.

We all have the desire to make a difference, take action, to do, be and want more for ourselves and others. Even if each of us had all the money in the world, we would still want to contribute and to live our lives giving to others, and receiving in return.

Enjoy your life and live each day to the fullest and funnest degree! The ups and downs are all part of the ride. Your destination is just to ride the next ride. So have fun and play along the way!

My final thought is a selfish one. I hope that in some way as you read and internalize the words on the pages within this book, you are inspired in some way to have fun and play more. Please pass along this inspiration and play with another today and every day. My favorite thing in life is to play, inspire others to play and to witness others at play. There is something magical, even spiritual, when people laugh, have fun and are truly enjoying themselves.

From the bottom of my heart and soul, I invite you to

support my purpose and yourself by creating a world in which we are all pretending, laughing and playing again. We all have the opportunity to create a fun-filled day and your fun and enjoyment will naturally inspire others, I promise. You DO make a difference. You are amazing, special and perfect! You are a part of everyone and everything else. When just a few of us start playing and having fun in life every day in every way possible, others will follow.

Come on, let's play Tag, Follow-the-Leader or simply Make Believe. There are so many ways you can spread play around the world! Write this down, stick it everywhere so you will always remember...

Every day in every way there is always an opportunity to PLAY!!

REFERENCES

Recommended Reading and Contributing Support and Inspiration

A Whole New Mind by Daniel Pink

Ask and It Is Given by Esther and Jerry Hicks, from the teachings of Abraham.

Biology Of Belief, The by Bruce Lipton

Born To Run by Christopher McDougall

Cash Flow For Kids by Robert Kiyosaki (game)

Crush It by Gary Vaynerchuk

Delivering Happiness by Tony Hsieh

Five Love Languages, The by Gary Chapman

Healthy At 100 by John Robbins

In the Meantime: Finding Yourself and the Love You Want by Iyanla Vanzant

Millionaire Mind, The by T. Harv Eker

Oh, the Places You'll Go! by Dr. Seuss

Play by Dr. Stuart Brown

Purple Cow by Seth Godin

Pursuit Of Happyness, The by Chris Gardner

Seth Material, The by Jane Roberts

Start With Why by Simon Sinek

Things That Make Us Smart by Don Norman

Think and Grow Rich by Napoleon Hill.

You Can Heal Your Life by Louise Hay

Trump The Art Of The Deal by Donald Trump

How To Win Friends and Influence People by Dale Carnegie

Your Wish Is Your Command by Kevin Trudeau

The Element: How Finding Your Passion Changes Everything by Sir Ken Robinson, Ph. D.

Recommended Viewing:

Justin Bieber: *Never Say Never* (Paramount Pictures)

The Secret (Prime Time Productions)

Taylor Swift Journey To Fearless (The Hub Productions)

Contributors

Dunnagan, Jan: Author of *You GET IT when you GET IT*
Kallman, Vicki: http://www.vickikallman.com/
Navarre, Blake: Father and comedian
Peck, Joan: http://www.bejeweled7.com/
Snead, Patrice: Visibility Consultant, Las Vegas, NV
Teal, Joyce A.: http://joyceateal.net/
Tyler, Pam: Las Vegas, NV

QUICK ORDER FORM

Email Orders: orders@InspirationBooksPublishing.com

Postal Orders: Inspiration Books, Darlene Navarre, PO Box 530063, Henderson, NV 89053, USA.

Please send the following books, disks, or reports. I understand that I may return any of them for a full refund---for any reason, no questions asked.

_____

_____

_____

Please send more FREE information on:

☐ Other Books   ☐ Speaking/Seminars

☐ Consulting   ☐ Add you to our mailing list

Name:_____

Address:_____

City:_____State:_____Zip_____

Telephone:_____

Email Address:_____

Sales Tax: Please add 7.75% for products shipped to California addresses.

Shipping by air:
U.S.: $4.00 for first book or disk and $2.00 for each additional product.

International: $9.00 for first book or disk and $5.00 for each additional product (estimate).

QUICK ORDER FORM

Email Orders: orders@InspirationBooksPublishing.com

Postal Orders: Inspiration Books, Darlene Navarre, PO Box 530063, Henderson, NV 89053, USA.

Please send the following books, disks, or reports. I understand that I may return any of them for a full refund---for any reason, no questions asked.

_____

_____

_____

Please send more FREE information on:

☐ Other Books   ☐ Speaking/Seminars

☐ Consulting   ☐ Add you to our mailing list

Name:_____

Address:_____

City:_____State:_____Zip_____

Telephone:_____

Email Address:_____

Sales Tax: Please add 7.75% for products shipped to California addresses.

Shipping by air:
U.S.: $4.00 for first book or disk and $2.00 for each additional product.

International: $9.00 for first book or disk and $5.00 for each additional product (estimate).

QUICK ORDER FORM

Email Orders: orders@InspirationBooksPublishing.com

Postal Orders: Inspiration Books, Darlene Navarre, PO Box 530063, Henderson, NV 89053, USA.

Please send the following books, disks, or reports. I under-stand that I may return any of them for a full refund---for any reason, no questions asked.

_____

_____

_____

Please send more FREE information on:

☐ Other Books   ☐ Speaking/Seminars

☐ Consulting   ☐ Add you to our mailing list

Name:_____

Address:_____

City:_____State:_____Zip_____

Telephone:_____

Email Address:_____

Sales Tax: Please add 7.75% for products shipped to California addresses.

Shipping by air:
U.S.: $4.00 for first book or disk and $2.00 for each additional product.

International: $9.00 for first book or disk and $5.00 for each additional product (estimate).

Made in the USA
Columbia, SC
19 January 2024

30675635R00136